PILOT'S GUIDE TO FLIGHT
EMERGENCY PROCEDURES

PILOT'S GUIDE TO FLIGHT EMERGENCY PROCEDURES

N. H. Birch AFR Ae S and
A. E. Bramson AFR Ae S

Doubleday & Company, Inc., Garden City, New York, 1978

Illustrations by A. E. Bramson

Library of Congress Cataloging in Publication Data

Birch, Neville Hamilton.
Pilot's guide to flight emergency procedures.

Edition of 1973 by A. E. Bramson and
N. H. Birch, published under title: Flight
emergency procedures for pilots.
Includes index.
1. Airplanes—Piloting. 2. Aeronautics—
Safety measures. I. Bramson, Alan Ellesmere.
Flight emergency procedures for pilots. II. Title.
TL710.B63 1978   629.132′5214
ISBN: 0-385-13544-0
Library of Congress Catalog Card Number 77–91556

Originally published in England under the title of
FLIGHT EMERGENCY PROCEDURES FOR PILOTS
American edition corrected and adapted 1978

Note to Readers

This book was originally published in Great Britain, where general aviation is remarkably similar to aviation in the United States. Some of the technical terms in British aviation are different from the American vocabulary, however, and in all possible cases, the text has been adapted to conform to American usage. Although the reader may occasionally detect a British flavor in the writing, this should in no way affect the comprehensibility of the book. Light aircraft flown in each country are often produced by the same manufacturer, and civil air regulations differ only in small details.

Editor

Preface

A newcomer to the world of flying may, at first glance, find little comfort or encouragement in the contents of this book. Yet it was with a view to giving confidence that we decided to write PILOT'S GUIDE TO FLIGHT EMERGENCY PROCEDURES in the firm belief that a knowledgeable pilot is best equipped to deal with an unscheduled incident.

How can a pilot deal with a failed landing gear if he is completely unaware of how it works? What are the chances of pulling off a damage-free forced landing when the pilot has not tried one since he was a student? If an engine fails while taking off in a light "twin" when is it safe to carry on around the pattern and when should one land ahead? It is knowledge of this kind that ensures safety and safety brings peace of mind.

Each chapter is divided into three parts. There is a story, in most cases fictitious but based upon fact, where the pilot does everything wrong. There is a section giving the correct procedure in step-by-step form, while Part III of the chapter provides background information based upon experience of the emergency together with subject revision for the benefit of those who learned to fly long ago.

One of the greatest insurances available to pilots is the ability to recognize, at an early stage, that which is abnormal. In most cases this is largely a factor of experience, but experience is a time-consuming commodity. Its absence can, to a large extent, be balanced by sound training, common sense and the ability to adopt instinctively the correct drill when faced with an emergency.

Few emergencies in an airplane are beyond cure. It is what happens after the onset of trouble that so often makes the accident. Statistics prove this to be the case. We earnestly hope that this book will help reduce the accident rate.

A.E.B.
N.H.B.

Contents

PILOT'S GUIDE TO FLIGHT
EMERGENCY PROCEDURES

CHAPTER 1

Forced Landing Without Power

PART I. THE SITUATION

John Smith had been flying for three years or more—odd Sundays, the occasional trip to France—nothing very ambitious. It had all been fairly uneventful until the day he invited his next door neighbors for a ride. The conditions were splendid: blue sky broken by a scattering of fair weather cumulus and only a gentle breeze. Then, three thousand feet above the Sussex countryside the engine suddenly stopped firing—no smoke, no rough running —nothing. Just silence as the propeller windmilled round. "Ah-ha! Carburetor icing!" announced our pilot friend with a confident grin as he pulled out the heat control. Nothing happened. "Lord, we've got a forced landing," he said in utter disbelief. "Can you see any smoke for a wind direction?" There was none—and since he had forgotten take-off direction there was nothing for it but to find a field and make a guess at the line of approach. His eyes wandered anxiously from the windmilling propeller to the left, but never once to the right where a large green field lay within easy gliding distance. "There's a likely one over on the left," he thought to himself, "few trees on the approach and a little orchard at the end. Must get close to it—can't afford to undershoot." By now he was gliding along the boundary of his selected field, almost over it in fact, so that when he did turn onto base leg it was only a matter of seconds before the approach was overflown and a hasty "S" turn followed to avoid the woods lying along the right-hand side of the field. Too late he woke up to the fact that he was high, very high. In near panic he clawed on full flap in one fumbling heave. Was he imagining it or were the flaps not very effective today? Then it dawned on him—he was downwind and it was too late to do anything about it.

The edge of the field flashed by as he pushed into a frantic dive, a last minute attempt at getting down. The ground came up, he held off then float—float—float: Would she never land? By now, half the field was behind him, then, relief at last—the wheels touched and they ran along the ground. "Brakes—must get the brakes on," he kept telling himself as the orchard raced towards him—filling the windshield, then—thump! they hit a small apple tree, the aircraft slewed around, coming to a halt with a minor dent on one wing and hardly another scratch. It was unbelievable.

Back at the club, John Smith and his neighbors were busy sinking scotch while the members crowded around. He was the center of attraction, an ace. After all, had he not pulled off a forced landing with hardly a mark to show for it? The CFI came in. He had just returned from the field with an engineer. "Been looking at it," he announced to the hushed clubroom. "You must be tired of life, Mr. Smith—you had left the fuel and ignition on." In some odd way, the silence that followed reminded John Smith of that moment of not many hours ago when his engine had failed.

PART II. THE PROCEDURE

It is an average day with moderate wind and broken cloud at 3,500 ft. The aircraft is on a cross-country flight over open terrain when, without warning, the engine fails.

Immediate Action

1. Hold the aircraft nose in the level attitude, thus conserving height while the speed is reduced to the best gliding value.

2. Trim the aircraft at best gliding speed. Too high or too low an airspeed will result in unnecessary loss of height.

3. Look for a good field taking into account size, apparent surface, distance from the aircraft and if possible, availability of a house or farm for after-landing help; but this is of less importance than the other considerations.

4. Look for smoke to confirm wind speed and direction. Alternatively the broken cloud may cast shadows on the ground and their movement will usually be within 15° of the surface wind which will back during the descent. In the absence of any wind indications, use the take-off direction for landing.

Planning the Pattern

1. Plan a normal pattern around the chosen landing area, avoiding complicated maneuvers. Never turn away from the field, which must be kept in sight at all times.

2. Select a 1,000 ft. point or area. This is the key to the success of the operation—yet its true function and position is very often misunderstood (see page 14).

3. Without delay turn towards the 1,000 ft. point. Assess the ground elevation by visual judgment.

4. Be prepared to adjust the flight path so that the aircraft will arrive over the point at 1,000 ft. above ground level (Fig. 1).

5. While gliding to the 1,000 ft. point try and find the cause of engine failure. The symptoms of the failure will often provide a good indication of the cause (see page 14). When the power loss is accompanied by smoke, vibration and unusual noise there has almost certainly been a mechanical failure. Fuel and ignition must be switched off immediately. Alternatively when the propeller windmills without mechanical noise it may be possible to restart the engine. Check—

A. Fuel pressure and operate fuel booster pump.

B. Fuel content. If possible, change to another tank.

C. Position of magneto switches.

D. Position of mixture control.

E. Try carburetor heat.

6. When time and conditions permit, send out a "Mayday," giving call sign, best known position and intention.

7. During practice, warm the engine with a good burst of power

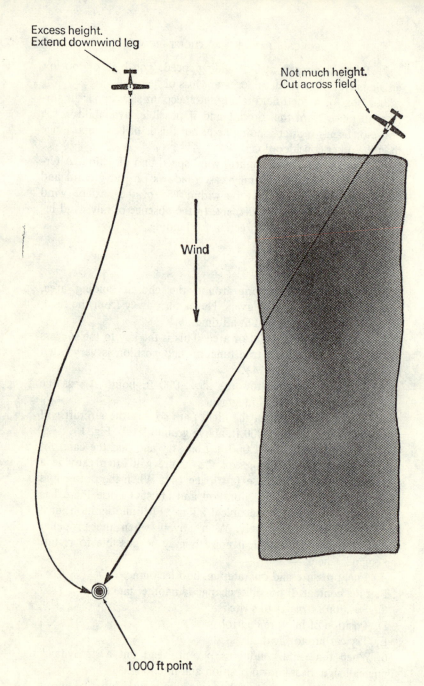

Excess height.
Extend downwind leg

Not much height.
Cut across field

Wind

1000 ft point

Fig. 1. Adjusting the glide towards the 1,000 ft. point according to circumstances.

at intervals of 500–1,000 ft. according to the outside air temperature.

8. Complete the usual downwind check list. These will include additional checks aimed at safe-guarding the occupants in the event of a bad landing—

B   Brakes off.
L   Landing gear up.
M   Mixture idle cut off.
P   Pitch coarse (simulate in practice; see page 11).
F   Fuel off.
I   Ignition off.
S   Seat belt tight.
D   Doors ready for quick release.

Note. Some aircraft become difficult to manage when the door is allowed to open slightly. At this stage pilot action should therefore be confined to unlocking rather than taking off the latch.

9. Maintain a close check on progress towards the 1,000 ft. point. Avoid dissipating height by gliding at the incorrect speed. Make full use of trim.

10. At the 1,000 ft. point turn onto base leg. Assess the strength of the wind by the amount of drift and adjust the base leg accordingly.

11. Aim to overshoot slightly thus ensuring that the field is within gliding distance.

12. When certain the field can be reached, lower the landing gear (if applicable; see page 13).
Lower 10–15° of flap.

13. Turn onto the approach and look out for obstructions that may have gone undetected. Adjust the landing path accordingly.

14. Use the flaps in stages to bring the touchdown point forward thus making the full length of the field available for deceleration. Full flap should be applied as soon as it is certain the field can be reached. The lower the touchdown speed the better.

15. Before landing turn off the battery master switch.

16. Avoid obstacles and land at the lowest possible touchdown speed.

17. During the landing run look ahead and avoid rough ground or obstacles.

18. Apply the brakes and bring the aircraft to a halt as soon as possible.

19. Take steps to safeguard the aircraft and, if possible, put someone in charge while telephoning the base airfield.

PART III. BACKGROUND INFORMATION

With the development of thoroughly reliable engines, the Forced Landing Without Power, once an everyday experience for pioneer aviators, has now become a rare occurrence. However the likelihood of a forced landing as a result of mechanical failure, remote as it may be, does not rule out the possibility of unexpected power loss due to pilot error and for this reason the emergency which forms the subject of this chapter should be fully understood; it should also be practiced at regular intervals. The benefits are obvious—

(a) ability to cope with the situation should it occur, and
(b) an interesting and enjoyable exercise which must improve both the pilot's general handling skill and his judgment.

Possible Causes of Engine Failure

These may be divided into two categories—
A. Mechanical.
B. Pilot mismanagement.

A. Mechanical

The chances of a major component failure (e.g. broken crankshaft, connecting rod, etc.) are remote and the most likely engine faults are as follows:

1. *Blown Cylinder-head Gasket* (i.e. the gas-tight seal between the cylinder and its head). This will produce a reduction in power accompanied by a distinctive sound not unlike that of a leaking exhaust system on a car. Usually it is possible to continue flying but a landing should be made as soon as possible since prolonged running with a leaking gasket can damage both the cylinder and its head.

2. *Mechanical Fuel-pump Failure.* This being the final link between fuel tank and carburetor, it follows that an inoperative me-

chanical fuel pump will cause the carburetor to run dry within a few seconds. The symptoms are easily recognized by a sudden and decisive loss of power, the propeller windmilling without unusual mechanical noise or vibration, the fuel pressure gauge reading zero. The remedy is simple. Switch on the emergency fuel pump.

3. *Fuel-line Blockage.* Either in the form of foreign matter in the fuel pipe or an air lock caused by incorrect use of the fuel selector. Symptoms are the same as in fuel pump failure. In each case the remedy is to augment fuel pressure by switching on the electric fuel pump. Should this have no effect, change tanks.

4. *Magneto Failure.* May take several forms. An electrical fault causing loss of spark is unlikely to occur in both magnetos simultaneously unless the ignition switch develops a short in flight and this is an even more remote possibility. Failure of one magneto will effect a small power reduction but even with fixed-pitch propellers this will probably go undetected by the pilot, hence the importance of a magneto check during the after-landing rundown.

Of more serious consequence is failure of the magneto drive. It is not unknown for the engine drive coupling to shear—when the magneto may continue to rotate, generating sparks and delivering them to the plugs at the wrong time. Symptoms are unmistakable. The engine will misfire to the accompaniment of violent shaking which is transmitted throughout the aircraft in a manner unlikely to be confused with rough running or carburetor icing. If the engine is allowed to continue running while in this condition very serious damage can result and immediate action must be taken to stop the misfiring. Again the remedy is simple—test the switches, then turn off the offending magneto. With the engine now dependent upon one ignition system an early landing must be planned.

5. *Detached or Faulty Plug Lead.* When only one lead becomes detached from its spark plug little if anything will be noticed by the pilot unless the lead makes contact with another plug. The design of ignition harnesses makes this highly improbable but in the unlikely event of it happening symptoms similar to magneto drive failure will occur. Here again the cure is to find the faulty ignition system, switch it off without delay, revise the flight plan and land as soon as possible.

6. *Sticking Valve.* To achieve power, during the compression and ignition strokes both valves in the cylinder head must be tightly closed. Occasionally, seizure of a valve in its guide, or a

broken valve spring, may allow a valve to remain open. In the case of an inlet valve, mixture will be pumped back through the carburetor in the reverse direction to normal flow, thus affecting carburetion to all cylinders and causing a general loss of power. In this case it is usually possible to remain in the air until an airfield is reached.

An exhaust valve which remains open during compression and ignition will allow mixture to be pumped into the exhaust manifold, when loud misfiring will be heard accompanied by rough running. This is not usually so violent as magneto drive failure but serious nevertheless. Prolonged running under these conditions may cause failure of the exhaust system with a risk of fire. Power should be reduced to the minimum possible and an early landing effected.

B. Pilot Mismanagement

PREFLIGHT

The best possible advice is "Know your aircraft." So often a forced landing has resulted from pilot ignorance, some of it inexcusable, occasionally because the unexpected has caught him off guard. Some of the most common pilot "traps" are as follows.

1. *Never Trust a Fuel Gauge.* It may work today. It may work tomorrow but that is no guarantee it will not tell a lie next week. Even when the aircraft is well known, never accept a gauge as working until its reading has been checked by visual inspection of the fuel tank. With some aircraft fuel cannot be seen from the filling point and in these cases the dipstick provided for the purpose should be used.

2. *Incorrect Use of Fuel Strainers.* The practice of ignoring fuel strainers before the first flight of the day is clearly a source of potential danger. However it is perhaps less apparent that misuse of the fuel strainers may create a hazard of another kind. There have been cases when the pilot has omitted to select fuel "on" before straining the tank. The resultant back pressure has gradually prevented further draining, thus giving the impression that the strainer has been closed correctly when in fact it is partly open. The pilot's first indication that a situation exists is when he be-

comes aware of what appears to be abnormal fuel consumption followed by a dry tank.

3. *Engine Seizure Resulting from Insufficient Oil*. Most engines, irrespective of age or design, lose oil, either through minor leaks, burning or negative "g" incurred during aerobatics. It therefore follows that an engine low on oil at the beginning of a flight may be dangerously low towards the end of the detail.

In extreme cases, shortage of engine oil will produce a complete seizure with potentially dangerous and invariably expensive results. The lesson is clear—check the oil level before flight.

The three areas for pilot negligence mentioned in the preceding text can all be avoided by elementary airmanship—

Never Fly Without First Completing the Outside Checks

DURING FLIGHT

1. *Carburetor Icing*. It should never be assumed at any time that conditions are such as to preclude the possibility of carburetor icing. The most likely range of outside air temperatures when icing may occur is generally quoted as between $+30°$ C and $-18°$ C. Correct use of the carburetor heat control is complicated by a number of variables and Chapter 10 deals with the subject in greater detail.

2. *Incorrect Use of the Mixture Control*. Will cause a decrease in power and overheating. Do not lean the mixture below the minimum flight level recommended in the operating manual. When one is fitted, make full use of the fuel/air ratio meter and never lean below the minimum setting which is usually "red lined." When there is no meter the mixture should not be leaned to the point where a loss of power and rough running is apparent.

3. *Mismanagement of Fuel*. Avoid running a tank completely dry. Should this occur there will often be evidence of "surging" as the remaining drops of fuel are drawn from the tank, followed by complete loss of power.

When changing tanks always turn the fuel selector through the positions detailed in the flight manual. If this recommends going from one tank to the other through the "off" position make a habit of so doing.

On some aircraft a particular tank is to be used for taking off and landing. If the manufacturer makes such a recommendation take it as certain that special reasons exist and follow their advice without exception. It is good practice to switch on the fuel booster pump when changing from one tank to another.

4. *Running Out of Fuel.* Possibly the most common cause of Forced Landing Without Power, running out of fuel, usually results from incorrect flight planning. With modern radio aids it is not usual for pilots to be uncertain of their position and the most likely cause when running short of fuel is either—

(a) reliance on the readings of an inaccurate fuel gauge, or
(b) failing to allow sufficient fuel for a weather deterioration and a possible diversion.

When it is clear that fuel will be insufficient to reach the destination a Forced Landing with Power (Chapter 2) should be attempted in the best available field on the basis that it is better to be able to choose a field under power, while you can.

5. *Misuse of Engine Controls.* It is not unknown for a pilot under stress to check for carburetor ice by mistakenly pulling out the mixture control, thus operating the idle cut-off. When an engine does fail, naturally the position of the mixture control is included in the checks for possible cause of power loss.

6. *Ignition Switches.* While it is remotely possible to accidentally knock off the ignition in flight most modern light aircraft have an ignition key and although the position of this will naturally be checked in the event of engine failure it is unlikely to be the cause of the trouble.

General Considerations When an Engine Fails

When notwithstanding all checks and preflight preparations the engine fails in the air, safe landing of a single-engine aircraft is affected by the following factors—

1. Extent of engine failure, i.e. partial or complete (in the case of a multi-engine aircraft failure of one engine presents quite different problems and these are dealt with in Chapter 5).
2. Type of aircraft and its handling characteristics.
3. Weather, particularly wind strength.
4. Nature of terrain below the aircraft.

5. Selecting the landing area.

6. Position of wheels in aircraft with retractable landing gears.

7. Amount of light at time of engine failure.

8. Altitude at time of engine failure.

1. *Extent of Engine Failure.* The procedure outlined in Part II of this chapter was based upon complete loss of power. Partial engine failure, i.e. when sufficient power remains to maintain height at a reduced speed, raises the question of whether to land immediately or seek a more suitable area. Over open country, however, it is usually better to ignore the limited power available and get the aircraft down in the first suitable field rather than fly on and risk complete failure when the ground below may be less hospitable.

2. *Type of Aircraft and Its Handling Characteristics.* The gliding characteristics of the aircraft must be fully understood as well as the effect of lowering flap and landing gear. An emergency is not the time to discover that application of full flap with the engine off results in a steeper than expected descent path.

When a constant-speed propeller is fitted, glide performance may be improved by selecting "coarse" pitch, this being the nearest equivalent to "feathering." During practice procedures coarse pitch should only be simulated, otherwise engine damage may result when opening the throttle at intervals.

3. *Weather and Wind Strength.* When the failure occurs in or above cloud a descent must be made away from known high ground. Full use should be made of the radio, since ATC may be able to guide the aircraft away from obstructions.

The descent through cloud must be made as quickly as possible because unless there is an alternative vacuum source or the gyro instruments are electrically driven, the artificial horizon, directional gyro and eventually the turn needle will cease to give reliable indications.

Appreciation of wind strength and direction is all important. It can mean the difference between success and failure when committed to a forced landing. Look out for smoke—which is the best indication of surface wind—but when none is available it is sometimes possible to use cloud shadows. Assuming the clouds to be at approximately 2,000 ft., wind direction will be some 15° less than the line of shadows.

4. *Nature of Terrain.* Obviously this will determine the selec-

tion of landing area available. When the engine fails while in sight of the ground it is simply a matter of choosing the best field, but a forced landing which begins above cloud will present the additional problem of terrain clearance mentioned under the previous subheading. When flying above cloud in a single-engine aircraft it is therefore prudent to keep a mental picture of the ground below by referring to the map at intervals.

5. *Selecting the Landing Area.* Of the many considerations likely to ensure a safe Forced Landing Without Power none are more important than the ability to judge height, distance and wind. To these must be added the intelligent selection of a suitable landing area. Unlike a Forced Landing with Power (Chapter 2) there will be no opportunity for close inspection of the approaches and surface of the chosen field; in fact an assessment will usually have to be made from a height of at least 2,000 ft. with nothing more than color and an overall impression for guidance. Obviously a large field, free of obstructions and landing into wind, would be a first choice although it is usually better to land uphill and across wind when these conditions prevail. Also the longest run may be preferable to landing into wind. The following notes will act as a guide when selecting a field from the air—

Qualities required
1. Large as possible.
2. Clear approaches.
3. As level as possible.
4. Good surface.
5. For preference near a farm or a house so that help may be obtained after landing.

Size is easy to determine from the air and major obstructions (power lines, trees, etc.) can usually be seen.

Level is not easy to detect until the later stages of the forced-landing pattern but small undulations are of little consequence.

Surface presents the biggest problem and this may be assessed as follows—

Grassland	Varying from dark green to brownish green according to dampness or dryness. Surface may be mottled.
Stubble	Generally buff color. At lower altitudes regular lines may be visible.

Ripe grain	Color varies between buff and golden brown according to type of crop. A distinctive wave pattern is set up by the wind, indicating its direction.
Young grain	Dark green, varying in shade.
Root crops	Regular lines visible, particularly when crops are young.
Ploughed fields	Dark red-brown, according to area. If no other choice, land with the furrows.
Marsh	Dark green with much darker areas. Streams and pools of water may be evident in the vicinity. A last resort.
Beach	Sand running within a few yards of the water's edge is usually firm enough to provide a good landing.

6. *Position of Wheels*. There has been some rethinking on this subject in recent years, primarily as a result of the almost universal adoption of the tricycle landing gear.

Tailwheel aircraft with retractable landing gear are now rare but in these cases it is still considered preferable to land on an unknown surface with the wheels retracted, thus avoiding the possibility of nosing over. When an aircraft—nose or tailwheel type—is for any reason landed with the landing gear retracted it is imperative to make contact in a flat attitude, even if the speed is high. The alternative is to reduce speed by holding up the nose and this invariably culminates in a tail-first touchdown or a rapid sink in the nose-up attitude, in each case causing more damage than is necessary to the aircraft.

With nosewheel aircraft it is now the practice to lower the landing gear, thus holding the fuselage and its occupants clear of minor obstacles which may have gone undetected at the time of selection. In any case the landing gear will very likely absorb the shock of landing on a rough surface and even if a collapse does occur there is little likelihood of injury, bearing in mind the low touchdown speed of most light twin- and single-engine aircraft. The landing will be dealt with later.

7. *Amount of Light at Time of Engine Failure*. This will obviously affect the ease or otherwise of completing the forced landing with minimum damage to the aircraft. The worst case is engine failure at night, although when there is a full moon it is usually

possible to see major obstacles and take avoiding action. Even the darkest night does not automatically mean disaster. Remember that at the low speeds associated with light aircraft there is no reason why the occupants should suffer injury provided the following precautions are taken—

A. Try and maintain a mental picture of the terrain below.

B. Turn into wind and trim at lowest airspeed consistent with safety, thus minimizing the effects of impact with trees, etc.

C. The landing light is of no value at 750 ft. and the battery will rapidly discharge if care is not exercised. Therefore only use the light during the final 150 ft. to avoid major obstacles and effect the best possible landing.

8. *Altitude at Time of Engine Failure* may or may not be an advantage. Five thousand ft. above unbroken cloud is a worse position to be in than 1,500 ft. below it and in sight of the ground. Other things being equal (i.e. visual contact with the ground) a minimum of 2,000 ft. is convenient, and cross-country flights should only be routed below that level for air traffic or weather reasons. Remember that when the altimeter is on QNH it is indicating altitude above the lowest forecast mean sea level for that area. Although a glance at the map will give some idea of ground elevation it is preferable to develop the ability of judging height above ground.

Safeguarding the Aircraft and Action to Be Taken After Landing

Having made a successful forced landing it would be inexcusable to incur damage to the aircraft through lack of precautions on the ground.

Whenever possible push the aircraft to a sheltered position, first checking the ground ahead for ruts, holes, etc. Position the aircraft into wind, put on the brakes and lock the controls. Cows have an affinity for elevators and rudders so it is advisable to place someone in charge of the aircraft while a telephone call is made to the base airfield or the destination.

Common Faults During Forced Landing Procedures

1. *The Pattern*. Avoid complicated patterns and try as far as possible to conform to the normal glide path (Fig. 1).

2. *Selection of the 1,000 ft. Area*. So often the correct position-

ing of the 1,000 ft. area is misunderstood yet its intelligent selection can be the difference between failure or success when committed to a Forced Landing Without Power.

Reject all complicated advice (e.g. "45° from the center of the field, etc.") because there is no time to play guessing games, trying to judge 45° in perspective unless the aircraft is directly over the field. This in any case is a difficult position from which to initiate a forced landing. The correct position of this vital 1,000 ft.

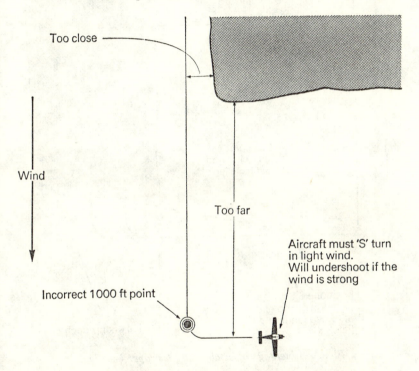

Fig. 2. Common fault in positioning the 1,000 ft. point.

point is simple to define. It is the beginning of the base leg, no more, no less. A common error in positioning is illustrated in Fig. 2 where it can be seen that the 1,000 ft. point is too far downwind and much too close to the final leg. Such a choice is likely to result in—

(a) a bad overshoot when the wind is light, necessitating last-minute "S" turns (which are to be avoided unless absolutely essential), or

(b) an irretrievable undershoot when the wind is strong.

The ideal 1,000 ft. point is shown in Fig. 3. From this position a

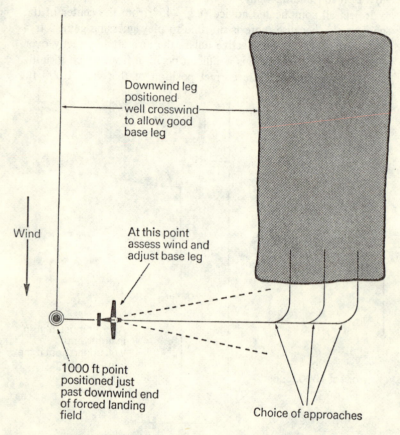

Downwind leg
positioned
well crosswind
to allow good
base leg

Wind

At this point
assess wind and
adjust base leg

1000 ft point
positioned just
past downwind end
of forced landing
field

Choice of approaches

Fig. 3. Advantage of establishing a proper base leg.

proper base leg may be developed which in turn will provide valuable information on wind strength which will be indicated by the amount of drift. The aim should be to overshoot slightly. It is always possible to lose surplus height, whereas nothing can be done about any undershoot when the engine has stopped. Adjustments can be made on the base leg and, in extreme cases when a serious overshoot seems likely, height may be lost in a sideslip away from the field (Fig. 4).

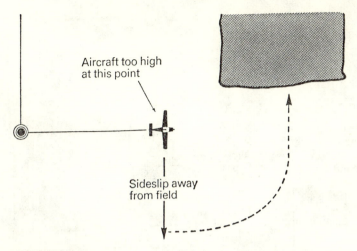

Aircraft too high
at this point

Sideslip away
from field

Fig. 4. Method of correcting a serious overshoot situation.

3. *Failure to Turn off the Fuel and Ignition.* There are two important reasons for turning off fuel and ignition and these actions must always be simulated during practice—

(a) reduction of fire risk in the event of damage during landing, and

(b) there must be no possibility of the engine bursting into life, so tempting the pilot to climb away. The next failure may occur when conditions for a forced landing are less favorable.

4. *Misunderstanding the Touchdown Point.* In more recent years it has become the practice to advise pupils to "land ⅓ of the way into the field." This is misleading and dangerous because unless the field is large, landing anywhere other than near the boundary is a potentially expensive luxury. By all means aim initially to land ⅓ of the way into the field but on the approach use the flaps to bring forward the touchdown point (Fig. 5).

5. *Damage During Landing.* It is of course impossible to check the surface of the field thoroughly before landing. Indeed the first close look at the touchdown area will occur during the final stages of the approach when these considerations should be born in mind—

(a) keep a sharp lookout for ruts, ditches, rocks or other obstacles and take avoiding action as necessary, and

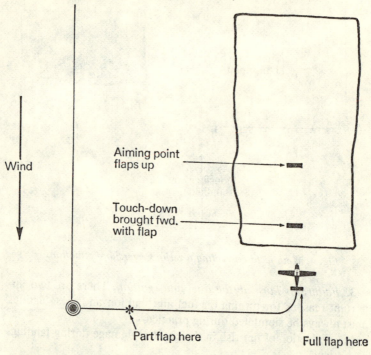

Fig. 5. Use of flap to bring touchdown point towards the field boundary, thus making available most of the forced landing field for the post landing run.

(b) aim to land at the lowest possible touchdown speed by prolonging the flare. It is important to get the tail down, even in nosewheel aircraft, the only exception being when landing with the landing gear retracted. Then it is advisable to make contact in the level attitude.

CHAPTER 2

Forced Landing with Power

PART I. THE SITUATION

What started as a little printing business in a garden shed had developed into a fair enough works with a modern building and a payroll of several hundred. Steve had good reason to be satisfied with the results of his hard work and after ten short years the progressive addition of modern machinery was followed by the acquisition of a small company aircraft. True, part of the reason for this addition to the family was a long nurtured ambition to become a pilot, but there was enough business on a national scale to justify a light plane and in any case just around the corner was the Common Market presenting new horizons.

That morning Steve had flown down to Exeter in answer to an inquiry from a prospective customer. It was an ideal opportunity to impress these potentially important people, for how often had a supplier visited them in his own aircraft? The deal was done and a jubilant Steve arrived back at the airfield ready for the flight back to Liverpool. Should he refuel? Of course he should but if he left now there would be time to get home before dark and this was important because he had never before flown at night.

It was not until well past Shawbury that he suddenly recognized his plight. The wind was far stronger than expected and the trip was taking longer than planned. It would be dark before he reached Liverpool and even this was in doubt because by now the fuel was running uncomfortably low. Even as he thought about it the light was fading and he was left with the chilling thought that the nearest airfield was probably beyond his near-empty tanks.

Just to the right was a large, green meadow, "big as a small airfield," he told himself. An obliging farmer was burning rubbish nearby and the smoke confirmed that he was more or less into wind, the very wind that had caught him unprepared. It all looked ideal for Steve and in an instant he had made up his mind—it was here in one piece or the chance of running out of fuel over the black waters of the Mersey. Or at best, his first attempt at a night landing and a lot of awkward questions to be answered later.

He turned downwind, hurriedly part-completed his checks, made a tight pattern around the field, fearful of losing it in the fading light, then came in to land. "Speed much too high—must get below the usual seventy knots—FLAPS!—nearly forgot full flap." He shot across the edge of the field, much too fast and rather high, the throttle closed and his legs trembling. At least he was in and it was a very large meadow.

It wasn't a bad landing and the ground was surprisingly smooth but by the time he saw it nothing could be done. The meadow was really two large fields divided by a low, iron fence and Steve went through it like an express train. He stood in the dusk examining the company aircraft: a broken nosewheel strut, the prop twisted, a battered left wing. "Three thousand dollars may cover the repairs," he thought to himself, "and all for a few gallons of gas and a little more daylight." Gas maybe, but need he have left Exeter so late with insufficient fuel? And having created the situation that followed need he have made such a mess of the Forced Landing with Power?

PART II. THE PROCEDURE

Due to shortage of fuel, deteriorating weather or failing light it has been decided to land as soon as possible before the situation becomes worse.

1. Reduce to low safe cruising speed and lower 10–15° of flap.

2. Select the best possible landing area and determine the wind direction as in a Forced Landing Without Power.

3. Check the approaches to the field from a height of 100 ft. or so, flying to the right of the intended landing path. Look out for high trees, power cables or any tall structure in line with the approach.

4. Maintain height and fly the length of the field checking for drift. At the same time determine if the field will be long enough for the landing and subsequent take-off. Look out for animals and any fixed obstacles.

5. If the visibility is poor set the directional gyro to "zero" while lined up with the landing direction.

6. After the field has been overflown climb to pattern height, remaining clear of cloud.

7. Maintain low safe cruising speed and fly around the pattern, opening the throttle slightly for the turns. Aim to keep the field in sight at all times. Position the aircraft on the base leg.

8. Having inspected the approach and overshoot from a safe height, plan another run over the field, this time for the purpose of checking the surface. Reduce to approach speed and lower the aircraft to about flare position. Look for holes, ruts, large stones or steep inclines, all of which must be avoided during the landing.

9. After the surface has been inspected climb to pattern height and provided the field is considered satisfactory fly downwind a little further than for a normal engine-assisted approach. Complete the check list—

B   Brake off.
L   Landing gear down and locked.
M   Mixture rich, carb heat cold (check for ice).
P   Pitch fine (or as recommended for type).
F   Fuel on, sufficient for overshoot, boost pump on.
S   Seat belt tight. Doors open (if type allows).

10. Establish a base leg and prepare for the landing which must be at the lowest possible speed consistent with safety. Use a little extra power for the turn onto the approach or if too high, depress the nose and gain five knots or so.

11. On the approach slacken the throttle nut and lower more flap leaving the final stage until certain of landing. Control the airspeed with the elevators and the rate of descent with throttle. Correct for drift in the usual way.

12. If the approach looks good for a landing lower full flap. Aim to cross the boundary of the field as low and as slowly as possible, always with safety in mind.

13. Look out for obstructions that may have been missed on the inspection run and as the touchdown point comes near reduce the power, closing the throttle completely just before landing.

14. Bring the aircraft to a halt, avoiding rough ground or anything likely to cause damage. Hold the stick back to keep the weight off the nosewheel (or to keep the tailwheel down when the aircraft is of the tailwheel type).

15. After the aircraft has stopped make no attempt to taxi before the ground ahead has been inspected on foot. If necessary, manhandle the aircraft to a more sheltered position, lock the controls and the doors, then report the incident to the base airfield or, if more convenient, the destination.

PART III. BACKGROUND INFORMATION

Avoiding the Situation

The factors generally regarded as likely to cause a Forced Landing with Power are as follows—

A. Shortage of fuel.
B. Approaching nightfall.
C. Uncertainty of position.
D. Unexpected deterioration of the weather.

An example of item A coupled with item B was given in Part I of this chapter. These days item C is usually associated with radio failure or misinterpretation of radio information. Unexpected weather deterioration has long been a part of flying but it is usually possible to divert or return to the point of departure. Clearly avoidance of "the situation" is a matter of correct flight planning. Never take off without sufficient reserves of fuel for a diversion; never leave insufficient time for the destination to be reached in daylight, unless there are night facilities available for the landing and the pilot's license includes a night rating; never allow a position uncertainty to continue. Make full use of the radar service or when outside radar coverage, use whatever VDF facilities exist near the required track.

Most radio navigational equipment incorporates a test button and pilots should form the habit of ensuring that their radio aids are working correctly. That rock-steady VOR needle may be good for the ego. It may also be stuck or the set may be off for some reason or other!

When the weather becomes unpleasant never carry on into conditions beyond the capabilities of the aircraft or the pilot. To turn back or reroute is not an admission of lack of skill. It is usually good airmanship unless of course the bad weather is known to be local in nature with good conditions ahead. However, when the point is reached where continuance of the fight may entail real risk, a Forced Landing with Power should be decided upon without delay, certainly while light and visibility remain and there is sufficient fuel to complete the procedure.

Low Safe Cruising Speed

It goes without saying that a reduction in speed will assist the pilot to think more clearly while planning the landing and selecting a field. When rain is present forward vision will be impaired. Some 10–15° of flap should be lowered when flying at low safe cruising speed because—

   (a) for any airspeed the nose will be lower, thus improving visibility forward (Fig. 6), and

   (b) since the flaps cause additional drag, power will be higher for any given airspeed and the increased slipstream will improve rudder and elevator response.

Because of the low speed, power should be increased slightly during turns.

When a constant-speed propeller is fitted, the rpm should be increased to 2,400 (or as recommended in the operating manual) thus allowing full use of the throttle should the situation warrant.

Selecting the Landing Area

Broadly speaking the considerations are very similar to those listed in the chapter on Forced Landings Without Power (page 12). However with the engine still running the pilot is therefore

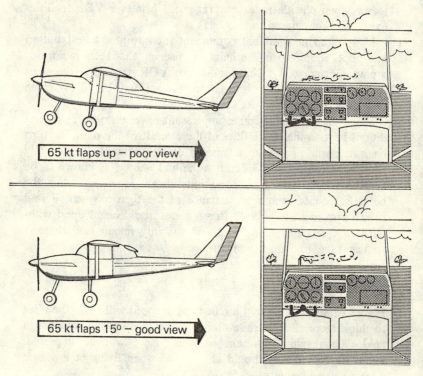

65 kt flaps up – poor view

65 kt flaps 15° – good view

Fig. 6. Use of part flap to improve the view ahead while flying at low safe cruising speed.

able to search for the best available landing area and having found it he may then make a detailed examination of the approaches and surface. To this extent he is better placed than when the engine fails.

In making the search notify ATC of the situation. They are often in a position to help, but when radio contact is lost and an airfield cannot be found choose the best field available—for preference one near buildings so that assistance may be obtained after the landing.

Landing Direction

While a landing into wind is always desirable there are occasions when the longest run would be better even when it is out of wind.

When there is an incline it is usually best to land uphill regardless of wind. The determination of wind direction is identical to that outlined on page 11.

Checking the Approach and Overshoot

Before any attempt is made to examine the surface of the field at low level the approach and overshoot paths must be checked from a safe height. In most aircraft it is difficult to see directly ahead and impossible to look directly below; therefore the examination should be made by lowering the aircraft to 100 ft. or so above the ground and flying to the right of the intended landing path (Fig. 7). Look out to the left and be quite satisfied that no telephone wires, power cables, high trees or tall structures are likely to endanger the approach. While over the field this is an opportunity to check for drift and generally assess the area for size and suitability. Drift at low levels can give the illusion of slipping or skidding during turns. Guard against this by checking the turn-and-slip indicator.

During the climb out, the overshoot area must likewise be checked for obstructions.

Checking the Surface

While the surface can only be checked at a low level and a low airspeed, neither height nor speed should be so low that the attention is fully committed to flying at the limit rather than seeing what lies along the projected landing run. Having proved the approach and overshoot on the previous run over the field, a descent may now be made with confidence.

Look out for stones, tree trunks, holes and ditches. And remember those low, frail-looking iron fences of the kind that afflicted Steve in Part I of this chapter! During the run across the field (again positioned to the right of the intended landing path) any animals present will normally move away from the selected landing area, but be prepared for them when coming in to land—like humans, animals are prone to change their minds.

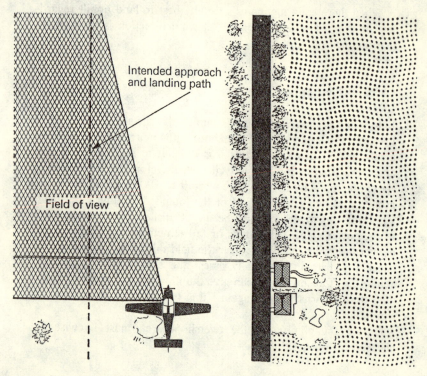

Intended approach
and landing path

Field of view

Fig. 7. Importance of flying to the right of the intended landing
path during the inspection runs over the field.

Bad Weather Pattern

The advantages of low safe cruising speed and the need for extra
power during turns have already been explained on page 23. It is
very easy to lose the selected field, particularly when visibility is
poor and the following advice should be of value to pilots who
may find themselves planning an unscheduled landing in a field.

1. Keep below cloud at all times.
2. During the first approach and run over the field set the directional gyro to "zero."
3. Check the drift and note whether it is port or starboard.
4. Find prominent features on the ground and use these to fix

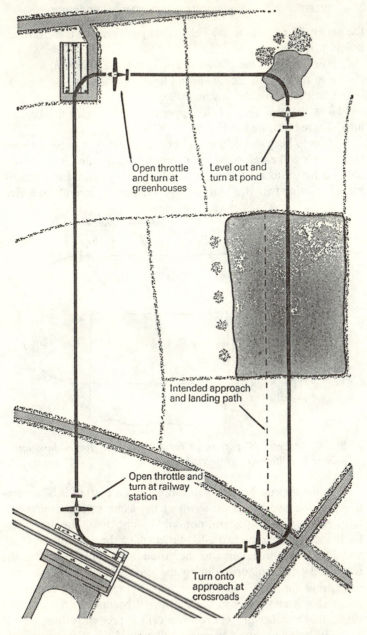

Open throttle
and turn at
greenhouses

Level out and
turn at pond

Intended approach
and landing path

Open throttle and
turn at railway
station

Turn onto
approach at
crossroads

*Fig. 8. Using turning points as an aid to keeping the field in view.
Pattern should be flown at low safe cruising speed.*

the pattern in relation to the field. Ideal positions for these turning points would be

(a) at the top of the climb out and before the first turn,

(b) at the start of the downwind leg,

(c) at the end of the downwind leg, and

(d) at the beginning of the approach, in line with the landing area. These illustrated in Fig. 8.

5. Aim to keep the field in sight or, at worst, just outside visual range. This will entail planning a compact pattern and it will probably be better to abandon the usual square pattern for a "race-track" utilizing two 180° turns (Fig. 9). For the aircraft to arrive

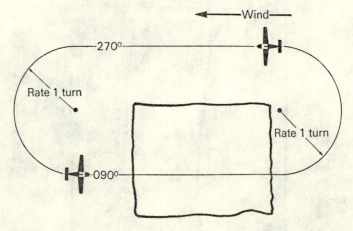

Fig. 9. "Racetrack" pattern to be flown around forced landing field in conditions of poor visibility.

back at the approach after completing such a pattern it is imperative that the two turns are flown at the same rate and airspeed. Drift can distort the pattern, not only by displacing the downwind leg but also during the two 180° turns which, because of the wind, will alter in radius relative to the ground. To compensate for the combined effects of drift during the downwind leg and the two turns, find the drift and its direction during the first inspection run, treble it and apply to the downwind heading in the opposite sense. Bad weather procedure when drift is present is illustrated in Fig. 10. It is important to make full use of the directional gyro when flying a bad weather pattern.

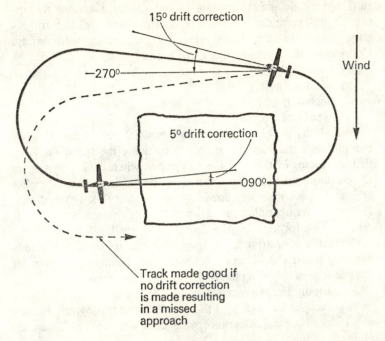

15º drift correction

—270º—

Wind

5º drift correction

—090º—

Track made good if
no drift correction
is made resulting
in a missed
approach

*Fig. 10. Compensating for drift in a strong cross wind. Broken
line shows effect on aircraft when no drift corrections are made.*

The Approach

The downwind leg will have to be extended a little to ensure a
good, straight-in approach and to allow sufficient time for both
pilot and aircraft to settle.

After turning onto the base leg, throttle back to, say, 1,500 rpm
and settle the aircraft at the usual powered-approach speed.
Lower 20° or so of flap, retrim and slacken the throttle nut to
allow easy power adjustment.

With the airspeed by now rather low a little extra power should
be added for the final turn in, although a "too high" situation can
be rectified by depressing the nose and adding five knots for
safety.

The technique of controlling the airspeed with the elevators and
the rate of descent with throttle is likely to produce the best re-

sults with single and twin piston-engine aircraft. Continue the approach until committed to the landing, then lower full flap and reduce speed to the lowest possible consistent with safety. Considerations governing this speed are—

(a) pilot ability,
(b) wind strength,
(c) degree of gustiness, and
(d) weight of aircraft.

Pilot ability may be cultivated by practicing slow flying with full flap and at a safe height, gradually reducing the speed until the first symptoms of the stall are recognized when back pressure on the elevators must be released and the power increased. A higher approach speed must be allowed for conditions (b), (c) and (d), and while the operating manual will be of guidance here there is no substitute for knowing the aircraft really well.

Correct use of trim is an important aid to holding a steady airspeed but it should be remembered that changes of power for the purpose of adjusting the glide path will upset the trim.

Avoid long, flat approaches with a lot of power. This is known as the "creeper method" and the penalty is poor forward visibility and reduced obstacle clearance when compared with a descending glide path (Fig. 11).

The Short Landing

If it has been executed correctly the last few hundred yards of the approach will be at a low airspeed with the aircraft "at the back of the drag curve," i.e. to fly more slowly will require higher power. Under these conditions the throttle must *on no account* be closed until the aircraft is in the flare position and ready to land; otherwise it will sink rapidly, probably stall and the subsequent landing will very likely be heavy enough to cause unnecessary damage (Fig. 12). With practice it is possible to position the actual touchdown with great accuracy, making contact with the ground within seconds of closing the throttle.

Pull-out Run

The emergency is not over until the aircraft stops rolling over the unknown ground. Keep a good lookout for rough areas ahead or

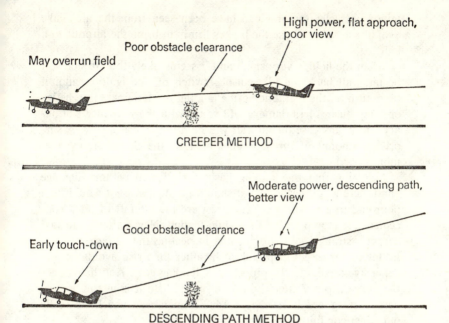

CREEPER METHOD

DESCENDING PATH METHOD

Fig. 11. Two methods of short landing approach. The descending path technique is preferable when a hedge or fence must be crossed before touchdown.

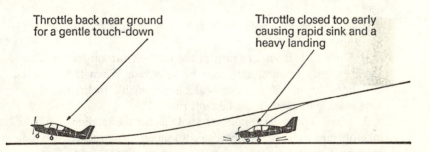

Fig. 12. The importance of maintaining a little power until the aircraft is in the flare position.

minor obstacles too small to have been seen from the air. Take avoiding action and use the brakes firmly to bring the aircraft to a halt.

When the field is very small and it seems likely the far side will be hit, pull back the idle cut-off, switch off the ignition and, if time, turn off the fuel. Should the landing run terminate in a hedge or some bushes less damage will result with the propeller stationary and in any case the aircraft will be rolling more slowly. A surprising amount of thrust is generated by the propeller, even at idling speed.

Assuming that the landing has been effected without damage (and there is no reason why it should be otherwise) it would be a poor end to a skillful performance were the aircraft to hit a concealed tree stump or the like while taxiing. Never attempt to taxi across a strange field without first inspecting the surface on foot. Better by far to get help and push rather than risk avoidable and expensive repairs to the propeller or landing gear. And having got the aircraft to a sheltered position on the field it is just as important to safeguard it (see page 14). Remember—you hope to fly out when conditions permit.

Taking Off from the Emergency Area

When the landing has been made on a disused airfield there will be no particular problems other than the possibility of animals grazing along the runways or farm equipment near the take-off path. The take-off must therefore be planned with more than usual care.

A strange field is another matter and the factors to consider are as follows—

1. *Surface.* It is vital to inspect the take-off run on foot so that small hazards (stones, etc.) can be removed. When the ground undulates, avoid—if possible—taking off uphill. Inclines and/or long grass will lengthen the take-off run.

2. *Wind.* The same conditions apply as for the landing. While a take-off into wind is usually ideal, a longer, clear run cross wind may be better. For take-off performance consult the operating manual.

3. *Obstacles.* Avoid having to clear high trees, etc., even if this means taking off out of wind. Remember that rolling friction on

an unprepared grass surface is considerably greater than for a hard runway and due allowance must be made when there are obstacles on the climb out.

4. *Weight.* Unless the field is very large, the lighter the aircraft the better—for obvious reasons—and it will be wise to remove all unnecessary load (suitcases, etc.) before flying the aircraft out solo.

5. *Length of Run.* Pace out the field and check with the operating manual to see if the aircraft will clear the far boundary under the prevailing wind conditions. When the take-off distance is marginal, taxi to the downwind end of the field then push the aircraft as far towards the boundary as possible so that every yard of the field is available. One yard may be the difference between flying out safely and hitting something at the other end.

6. *Use of Flap.* Most operating manuals claim shorter take-off runs and steeper climb paths when optimum flap is set. Measured tests tend to reveal that with most light aircraft the benefit is more psychological than real. However when 20° or so of flap is used the aircraft may be firmly rotated at a slightly lower than normal speed and provided the airspeed is held to a low value the climb path will be a little steeper. Here again, it is a case of getting to know your aircraft by practicing short take-off techniques.

CHAPTER 3

Engine Failure During and After Take-off (Single-engine Aircraft)

PART I. THE SITUATION

"They make such a big deal out of all these checks it's a wonder to me some people ever fly," commented Bill to a golfing friend as they taxied to the holding point. Then without pause, no run-up, no check list, no check to see if the approach was clear, Bill turned onto the runway and took off. True the electric fuel pump was off but that was of no consequence to Bill. And equally true the tank selected for take-off was all but empty. This meant nothing to Bill either because check lists were a "big deal" and this included a visual check of the fuel tanks before entering the aircraft.

At about three hundred feet the engine spluttered, then stopped. Ahead lay a small wood and to the left, wreathed in low-lying smoke, stood a factory, hopeless for a forced landing. Some 45° to the right was a clear area made up of biggish fields divided by thin hedges but Bill had already decided to get back to the airfield because, as he said afterwards, "it would have been more convenient" and "I thought I could make it."

In the racing seconds that flashed across Bill's mind the value of preflight and cockpit checks stood out in stark relief. At least he had the presence of mind to switch off the ignition and turn off the fuel.

Out of the corner of his eye he caught sight of the airfield, a very long way to the left. By now they were getting rather low and every instinct urged him to hold up the nose and tighten the turn but this was a different Bill and whatever his shortcomings he had no intention of spinning in.

Within sight of the airfield they ran out of height and landed in a rather liquid part of a sewage farm—it was all rather appropriate. After all there need not have been an engine failure and there was a good landing area available if only he had looked more carefully. Now the airplane was seriously damaged, Bill had a sprained wrist and a fractured rib and his friend swore he would stick to golf in future.

PART II. THE PROCEDURE

BEFORE LIFT-OFF

Shortly before lift-off the engine fails. Carry out the following actions.

1. Close the throttle.
2. Brake firmly.
3. At the same time switch off the ignition, turn off the fuel and pull back the idle cut-off.
4. If the aircraft seems likely to run out of runway and there is no overshoot area beyond, turn onto the grass.
5. If necessary take violent avoiding action.

AFTER TAKE-OFF

At a height of about 300 ft. the engine fails. Carry out the following actions.

1. Adopt the gliding attitude.
2. Close the throttle.
3. Look through an arc of some 60° left and right of center and select the best available forced landing area.
4. Avoid obstacles by making gentle to medium turns.
5. Only if time permits, select another fuel tank.

If the engine will not restart—

6. Switch off the ignition, turn off the fuel and pull back the idle cut-off. Raise the landing gear if it is a tailwheel type, otherwise leave the wheels locked down.

7. Delay using flap until it is certain the landing area can be reached. If there is a risk of overshoot, sideslip to increase the rate of descent but prevent the speed building up.

8. Just before landing unlatch the cabin door(s).

9. **Never attempt to turn back to the field.**

PART III. BACKGROUND INFORMATION

Likelihood of Engine Failure During Take-off

The developed modern engine has reached quite remarkable standards of reliability and it is rare for power failure to occur at any phase of flight, even during take-off when maximum power is being used. Isolated cases of engine failure during take-off that do occur are invariably the result of careless or non-existent preflight checks or check lists. The former were dealt with in the chapter on Forced Landing Without Power (page 8) and check lists really are vital. The true value of this advice would certainly be appreciated were the emergency to occur and the aircraft finish the take-off in, say, a ditch. The occupants would have good reason to be thankful that the seat belt had in fact been tightened during the "Seat Belts and Doors" check which forms part of these check lists.

Since an early engine failure may provide an opportunity to land ahead and still remain on the runway the practice of only using part of the available take-off run must be avoided.

Problems to Be Faced

The circumstances of an engine failure during take-off make it apparent that the pilot should be able to take actions that are not only correct but also instant. In most activities it has long been recognized that complex functions may be performed without conscious effort when they have been practiced to the point where they become automatic, e.g. the way a typist can use her machine without watching the keys, or a pianist can play at a speed beyond deliberate thought-controlled action. Many emergency aspects of flying depend upon the success of time-limited actions which are only attainable when they have been perfected in the form of well-practiced drills. At no time is this more true than during an engine failure on what is perhaps the most critical phase of flight, the take-off. The pilot wishing to ensure himself against the consequences of an emergency, with little time to spare, should practice the safety drills, learn the location of every switch and control in the aircraft and be able to find them without thinking but—remember—prevention is better than cure.

Engine Failure Before Lift-off

During the early stages of the take-off run it is standard practice to scan the engine instruments, checking that the expected rpm are being achieved and that temperatures and pressures are "in the green," i.e. within normal limits. It is a check to be taken seriously and *not* dismissed as a mere formality for this is the time when zero oil pressure or a temperature "pegging the needle" may be the prologue to complete or partial engine failure.

In the very unlikely event of power failure due to an aircraft fault nothing should be allowed to jeopardize the safe abandonment of the take-off. The fault may be intermittent and a failed engine that bursts into life while trying to stop the aircraft running off the airfield can only add to the problem. Therefore at the first sign of engine malfunction the throttle must be closed without delay.

Light aircraft field performance is such that when the abandoned take-off terminates in a hedge or over rough ground little airframe damage and no injury to the occupants need occur. However the risk of fire must always be taken seriously. It is best minimized by switching off the ignition, turning off the fuel and pulling back the idle cut-off. These actions must be developed as a drill so that, if the time ever came, they would be completed without thought while the brakes were applied and action was taken to avoid collision with objects on the ground.

When it seems imminent that the runway will be overrun turn onto the grass in an effort to increase rolling friction and shorten the deceleration period. At one time pilots were advised to retract the landing gear as an additional means of stopping the aircraft but modern thinking is that a tricycle landing gear will best protect the aircraft and its occupants when it is in the "down" position.

The ground stability of an aircraft with a tricycle landing gear is very considerable and the pilot should be prepared if necessary to make drastic changes of direction in order to prevent the aircraft from departing the airfield or hitting an obstruction. Minor damage to the landing gear is preferable to a written-off aircraft.

The foregoing should not be interpreted as meaning that engine failure during the take-off run must of necessity prove dramatic; quite the reverse. Indeed, on all but the smallest airfields it should be possible to abandon a take-off and stop a light aircraft without damage or injury.

Engine Failure After Take-off

All the safety considerations mentioned under the previous heading apply after the aircraft has left the ground but there are of course additional problems and the actions to be taken are affected by the following factors.

    A. Height above ground at the time of engine failure.

    B. Nature of the area ahead.

    C. Type of aircraft.

    D. Wind strength.

    E. Amount of light.

Such are the variables involved that it is only possible to give general guidance.

Height Above Ground. It does not follow that an abundance of height is an advantage when the engine fails. There may be open fields just outside the airfield perimeter and a built-up area beyond. It is therefore best to consider factors A and B together.

When the engine fails immediately after lift-off the aircraft may not have attained optimum gliding speed and there will be no alternative to lowering the nose and landing ahead, probably on the airfield unless it is very small. Assuming the airfield boundary has been crossed and the engine failure occurs at a height of several hundred feet there should be time to scan left and right of the take-off heading within a combined arc of 120° or in other words 60° either side of center (Fig. 13). While it is usually possible to

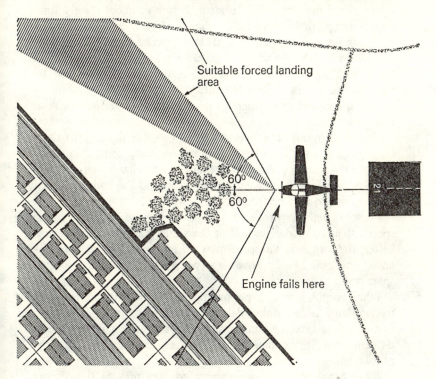

Fig. 13. Use of the 60° scan to find a safe landing area.

put the aircraft down in open country with little damage, buildings and power lines must, for obvious reasons, be avoided at all cost, even when the alternative is a landing in the trees. There have, in fact, been cases when even quite large aircraft have been put down between two lines of trees, allowing the wings to take the shock, the occupants being able to escape without serious injury.

Remember that only seconds remain for a landing area to be selected while the safety checks are completed.

In principle a 180° turn back to the airfield should never be considered. The danger of turning while descending near the ground is a natural desire to hold up the nose and add rudder in order to reach the field—ideal conditions for a spin from which there can be no recovery, because of insufficient height. The true nature of the problem may best be illustrated by a few simple figures. Bear in mind that in a medium turn of about Rate 2 time required to go through a heading change of 180° is 30 seconds. In that time the average light aircraft will descend some 500–600 ft. To this loss of height must be added a margin to cover the distance back to the airfield. The gliding turn could of course be tightened to a Rate 3 or 4 but safety would then demand an increase in airspeed and a higher rate of descent would result. And this leads to factor C.

Type of Aircraft. The importance of knowing the aircraft thoroughly has already been stressed in previous chapters. This emergency is no exception. The pilot should know what his aircraft will tolerate, how it will react when pushed beyond the limit and what can be done to recover from the new situation.

Modern high-performance monoplanes have higher stalling speeds than older designs but at the same time they also have a better lift/drag ratio and so display an improved gliding performance. This could be an advantage when trying to reach an open space some distance away.

Whatever the aircraft type, practice the drills and how to attain the optimum glide without delay. Learn how the aircraft behaves in medium and steep gliding turns and get some idea of the rate of descent during these maneuvers. These exercises can be practiced at a height.

Wind Strength. While a strong wind may prevent the aircraft reaching an ideal landing area ahead, it will at least reduce ground speed and the eventual touchdown speed. When impact is unavoidable its effects will be minimized in proportion to wind strength. For example, a 20 kt. wind will reduce a 50 kt. impact (airspeed) to 30 kt., hardly sufficient to cause serious injury to the occupants unless the pilot has contrived to fly into a brick wall!

The Landing. Only when it is certain the chosen landing area can be reached should the flaps be fully lowered. If an overshoot then seems likely the rate of descent may be increased by sideslipping but remember that unless the nose is held up as the wing is lowered the airspeed will increase and this in turn will cause the aircraft to float during the flare.

If the type permits, open the door(s) to ensure safe exit in the event of a heavy landing. Some types of aircraft become difficult to control when the door is allowed to open, but it is at least advisable to unlatch the door. When the design is known to be sensitive to door opening this may be delayed until the "round-out" but impaired flying characteristics are preferable to being unable to leave the aircraft when the door has jammed following a heavy landing.

Aim to touch down at the lowest possible speed. After the landing apply the brakes firmly. At this stage speed is the enemy and it is no time to worry about tires or even the landing gear itself. Therefore if the situation warrants, take violent avoiding action.

Amount of Light. The advice given so far is related to engine failure in daylight. At night all the considerations mentioned will apply and although darkness must obviously add a serious difficulty to the procedure, built-up areas are usually well lighted at night and can therefore be avoided. Alternatively when the environs are well known, lighted buildings will aid the recognition of likely landing areas.

At night it is particularly important to make a "Mayday" call if at all possible.

The landing light will assist during the final descent and the actual touchdown.

Practicing Engine Failure After Take-off

While the message throughout this book is "Proficiency through practice" a word of warning must be introduced here. Some engines have better throttle response than others and there have been cases when an engine failure has been simulated followed by a well-positioned glide into an open area. If, however, putting on the power is left to the last second most pilots have a natural tendency to slam open the throttle and it is not unknown for the engine to falter—when a real forced landing is almost bound to follow. It has happened. Then again carburetor heat, if applied, will inhibit throttle response. The moral is clear: It is not necessary to count the blades of grass in order to prove success.

CHAPTER 4

Engine Failure During and After Take-off (Multi-engine Aircraft)

PART I. THE SITUATION

"There's nothing to flying twins," said the smooth dealer who had just sold John a rather nice second-hand Twin Comanche. And of course he was right in so far as there is nothing to doing anything —when you know how. "I'll show you the flight controls and give you two or three hours, then we fill in this little form here and get a multi rating on your Private Pilot License." It all sounded fine to John, who by the way had hitherto flown nothing more potent than a Cessna 150.

It was all done one morning, three hours in the airplane including the test, then a somewhat bewildered John found himself the owner-driver of a fast, complex mini-airliner which was more than a little beyond him because the gap between a Cessna 150 and any light twin cannot be bridged in three hours, certainly not by a pilot of his very average ability.

On his second solo flight John fumbled. What he really meant to do was reduce the starboard throttle setting and bring it into line with the port engine. Instead he had hold of the mixture control and was unable to fathom why it made no difference to the manifold pressure on the right-hand engine. It seems inconceivable that anyone would move an engine control back to the stops during the climb out but John was confused and he did just that, the engine stopped and the airplane immediately swung to the right. "Keep straight at all costs," he told himself after an initial attempt with the wrong rudder. For a few seconds the situation was under control, then John noticed he was losing height. Without thinking to open up the live engine he lifted the nose— 115–110–100–90 mph—that swing to the right was developing again and so was panic.

Ahead lay a golf course. John took one look at its long, inviting fairways and gave in. Back with the throttles, a gentle turn and he was heading in with no thought of lowering flap or the landing gear, just an urge to get his "uncontrollable" airplane safely on the ground in one piece.

In the belly landing that followed surprisingly little damage was done to the Twin Comanche or the golf course. They gave him a double scotch, told him to sign the visitors' book, then phoned his wife. John was a silent and wiser man during the drive home. True he did not really understand why it had all happened but one thing was certain: He would get some proper instruction before flying his twin again.

PART II. THE PROCEDURE

Engine Failure Below V_{mca} (Minimum Control Speed. Take-off)

During the take-off run an engine fails before attaining V_{mca}. Take action as follows.

1. Close the throttles to both engines.
2. Keep straight.
3. Brake firmly.
4. At the same time switch off the ignition, turn off the fuel and pull back the idle-cut-off controls.
5. If the aircraft seems likely to run out of runway and there is no overshoot area beyond, turn onto the grass.
6. If necessary take violent avoiding action.

Engine Failure After Take-off but Below V_2 (Safety Speed)

Shortly after lift-off but before V_2 has been attained an engine fails. Take action as follows.

1. Prevent yaw, if necessary using aileron to assist rudder.
2. Lower the nose and maintain airspeed.
3. Identify the failed engine. "Dead leg—Dead engine."
4. If above minimum control speed, feather the dead engine, raise the landing gear, allow the speed to build up, then climb away.
5. When direction cannot be maintained, leave the landing gear down, reduce power on the live engine and if sufficient runway remains ahead, lower the flaps and land in the usual way.
6. If the airfield has been departed look through an arc of some 60° both left and right of center and select the best available forced landing area.
7. Avoid obstacles by making gentle to medium turns.
8. If time permits advise ATC of the situation.
9. If the chosen landing area is outside gliding distance use the live engine to reduce the rate of descent. Power must never be added to the point where direction cannot be maintained.
10. When certain of reaching the forced landing area—
    (a) close the throttle,
    (b) switch off the ignition,
    (c) turn off the fuel, and
    (d) pull back the idle cut-off controls.
11. Apply flaps as required, lowering them fully for the landing.
12. Just before landing, open the cabin door(s).
13. **Never attempt to turn back to the field.**

Engine Failure After V_2

The aircraft has become airborne, then shortly after reaching V_2 an engine fails. Take action as follows.

1. Prevent yaw, if necessary using aileron to assist rudder.
2. Maintain safety speed, if necessary by lowering the nose.
3. Identify the failed engine. "Dead leg—Dead engine."
4. Raise the landing gear if not already retracted, feather the

propeller on the failed engine, then switch off its ignition, turn off its fuel and pull back its idle cut-off.

5. Check for fire and if required operate the extinguisher.

6. Climb at the recommended single-engine climbing speed (blue line speed), checking the temperatures and pressures on the live engine for signs of strain.

7. Complete the pattern, advise ATC of your circumstances and prepare for a single-engine landing. (This is described in Chapter 6 on page 62.)

PART III. BACKGROUND INFORMATION

For practical purposes there is little difference between failure of one engine on a "twin" and failure of two engines on one side of a "four." In so far as the loss of one engine on a "twin" represents a power decrease of 50 per cent, while one engine failed on a "four" is a reduction of only 25 per cent, the latter is a less serious situation. However, although the title of this chapter includes the term "multi-engine aircraft," for convenience all the explanations are confined to aircraft with two engines arranged in the conventional layout, i.e. port and starboard of aircraft center.

Failure of an Engine During Take-off Before Attaining V_1

An aircraft accelerating during take-off will reach a speed and a point down the runway beyond which it will not be possible to abandon the take-off and stop within the remaining distance. This is known as **decision speed** or V_1. Beyond that speed a pilot is committed to the take-off or he may attempt to abandon it in the knowledge that he will depart the end of the runway and possibly the airfield itself. However, while the V_1 concept is of prime importance to large, high-performance transport aircraft it does not apply to airplanes to 12,500 lbs. maximum weight or less. Readers of this book will most likely be concerned with the operation of aircraft of this class, and to them the most important factors are whether the engine has failed while still on the ground or after lift-off.

Failure of an Engine Before Lift-off

Whether or not the take-off should be abandoned will depend upon—
  (a) how much take-off distance remains, and
  (b) whether or not the aircraft can be kept straight with maximum power on one engine.

Consideration (b) is a matter of rudder power which in turn depends upon airspeed and this will be more fully explained in the following paragraphs. At this stage it is sufficient to say that the minimum speed at which the aircraft can be held on a required heading against the full power of the live engine is quoted in the owners manual (V_{mca}) and this must be regarded as the "Go/No Go" on even the largest airfields while distance may be the deciding factor on more modest take-off runs. Here again the owners manual will give details of take-off performance under varying circumstances and these should be fully understood.

Possibly the worst case is engine failure below minimum control speed (to be explained later) while taking off from a small airfield. The position is that the power loss has occurred when the aircraft is going too fast to stop within the confines of the runway, but not fast enough to lift off and climb away with safety. Obviously the aircraft has to be stopped with as little damage as possible. The question is, how?

While it was once the practice to advise retracting the landing gear in a determined effort to stop the aircraft, present-day thinking is that modern brakes are very effective and tricycle landing gear allows full application of brakes without the risk of nosing over. Furthermore a tricycle landing gear in the "down" position will offer good protection to the occupants, holding them clear of rough ground and minor obstacles. In any case many aircraft have a built-in safety device which prevents the landing gear being inadvertently retracted while on the ground so there can be no question of raising the wheels in an emergency.

Assuming the failure occurs while operating out of a small airfield, it must be recognized that the take-off area will be overrun. It is best to aim for a hedge or small bushes; these will bring the aircraft to a halt with little damage. Impact can still further be reduced by stopping the live engine. The usual fire precautions apply (ignition and fuel off, idle cut-off operated).

Failure of an Engine After Lift-off

Before considering the problem to be faced in this emergency it is important to be quite clear about the forces involved when an engine fails on a twin-engine aircraft. In normal flight total thrust may be regarded as acting through the aircraft's center line and balanced by total drag. When an engine fails all thrust is then concentrated on the side of the live motor. Furthermore while ceasing to contribute thrust the failed engine, with its now windmilling propeller, will itself cause drag and, in effect, move total drag away from the aircraft's center line (Fig. 14). Put another way,

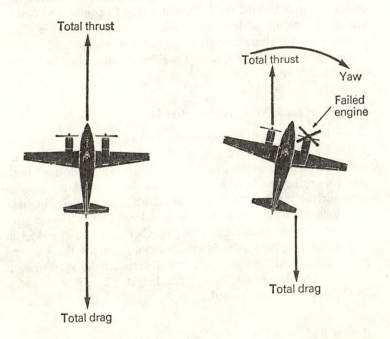

Fig. 14. Engine failure on a twin-engine aircraft. Total thrust and total drag move away from the center line and cause a yaw towards the dead engine.

when an engine fails and the aircraft is in **asymmetric flight,** total thrust and total drag diverge. If the forces illustrated in Fig. 14 are regarded as lengths of string attached to a model aircraft, then pulled in the directions indicated a swing towards the dead engine is bound to follow.

Thinking back to early training one of the first demonstrations in the air was entitled "Further Effects of Controls" when it was shown that the application of rudder caused yaw and yaw in turn produced roll when the nose would follow the lower wing into a spiral dive below the horizon. Failure of an engine on a twin will engender a similar chain of events to harsh application of rudder in the direction of the dead motor. The amount of yaw resulting from engine failure will depend upon—

(a) power of the live engine, and

(b) design of the aircraft, particularly the distance between the center of thrust and the aircraft's center line. Condition (b) determines the amount of leverage available under asymmetric flight conditions and aircraft with widely spaced engines will suffer greater yaw effect than those with engines installed close to the fuselage center line.

Controlling the Effect of Asymmetric Thrust

If asymmetric thrust is responsible for the yaw that starts the roll/spiral dive chain of events then clearly the yaw must be prevented at all costs if a disaster is to be avoided. Throttling back the live engine would of course remove the offset thrust responsible for the yaw but then the aircraft would lose height, perhaps at a time when there was no height to lose. Engine failure after take-off is indeed such a time. On the other hand use of rudder in opposition to yaw will maintain direction, prevent the roll and avoid the potentially dangerous spiral dive. At the same time it will allow the live engine to maintain height. There is, however, a limiting factor—the airspeed.

Use of Rudder in Correcting Yaw

On the principle that all flying controls are only as effective as the airflow over them it follows that as airspeed decreases the rudder will progressively lose its power to balance asymmetric thrust, until a speed is reached where full rudder must be applied to maintain direction. Any further reduction in airspeed will result in asymmetric thrust overpowering corrective rudder when the usual yaw/roll/spiral dive sequence would develop. The effectiveness of the rudder in dealing with asymmetric thrust depends upon rudder area and its distance from the aircraft's center of gravity; the longer the rear fuselage, the greater the leverage through which the rudder can exert its balancing force.

To some extent the use of rudder to maintaining direction after an engine failure may be assisted by aileron. Up to 15° of bank towards the live engine can be beneficial but excessive bank will adversely affect the ability of the aircraft to climb under marginal conditions.

Critical Speed

For any given conditions when full rudder has been applied to maintain direction against the yawing effect of the live engine the aircraft is said to have reached its **critical speed.** This is effected by the amount of power set on the live engine: The higher the power, the faster the airflow required by the rudder to balance yaw. It therefore follows that any operational factor calling for more power (heavy load, drag from landing gear, flaps, windmilling propeller, etc.) will raise the critical speed.

Critical Engine

While some twin-engine aircraft are fitted with opposite rotating propellers, usually they turn in the same direction. In these cases one engine will produce a slightly higher critical speed than the other but since the difference amounts to little more than a few knots there is no need for the pilot to fully understand the aerodynamics involved. In any case, all important speeds relating to asymmetric flight are based upon failure of the worst or **critical engine.**

Minimum Control Speed After Take-off (V_{mca})

Having revised the reader's knowledge of asymmetric flight it is now opportune to relate this information to the take-off, a phase of flight when maximum power is being developed by the live engine and a low airspeed is curtailing the effectiveness of the rudder. The critical speed under these very adverse conditions is known as V_{mca}, i.e. **minimum control speed** in the **airborne configuration.** The figure quoted in the operating manual will have been determined from tests under the following conditions—

(a) aircraft at maximum take-off weight,
(b) live engine at maximum power,
(c) failure of critical engine,
(d) propeller windmilling on the dead engine,
(e) landing gear not yet retracted, and
(f) flaps at the take-off setting.

When conditions (a) to (f) apply V_{mca} leaves no margin for error. It is without qualification the minimum speed at which direction can be maintained. Indeed as an operating figure for take-off safety purposes it is of little value. Instead it is the practice to use a slightly higher figure called V_2 **(take-off safety speed).** The safety speed quoted in the operating manual will take into account all the factors listed for minimum control speed with the addition of a safety margin to allow for—

(g) element of surprise,
(h) pilot of average physique and ability, and
(i) ability of the pilot to maintain control without retrimming, i.e. with the application of rudder and aileron only.

V_2 should therefore be regarded as a safe speed that must be attained as soon as possible during take-off; otherwise it may be difficult to maintain direction in the event of an engine failure.

Identifying the Failed Engine

The title of this section may read like a case of stating the obvious, yet experience has shown that a pilot acting under the stress of a power failure may react to the situation by closing down the live engine. On the face of it the suggestion that any pilot should, for example, feather the port propeller after the starboard engine has failed may sound like some kind of flying joke but the true likelihood of this happening is apparent to anyone regularly testing pilots for their multi-engine ratings.

On a twin-engine aircraft identifying the failed engine is simply a matter of checking the yaw, then saying out loud, "Dead leg—Dead engine." This means that the leg checking the yaw will be doing all the work (in some cases quite hard work) while the other leg is relaxed, inactive or to use the word in the check phrase, "dead." And the dead engine is adjacent to the pilot's dead leg.

Failure of an Engine Below V_2

Although in these cases the engine failure may have occurred below V_2 or safety speed this does not automatically mean that a forced landing is unavoidable. Provided minimum control speed has been reached, very prompt action will enable the aircraft to accelerate to safety speed. For example, the difference between minimum control and safety speed (V_{mca} and V_2) on a PA 30 Twin Commanche is only seven knots. Furthermore there is a body of opinion that favors holding the aircraft on the ground until it has accelerated to minimum control speed, and provided the available take-off run is long enough there is a lot to be said for the practice. After lift-off no attempt should be made to force the aircraft into the climb; rather it should be allowed to accelerate to V_2 while still near the ground. Most modern light twins will rapidly accelerate through V_2 and attain their climbing speed but a failure following a low-speed lift-off may mean that the direction cannot be maintained with full power on the live engine. At an average-sized airfield it will often be possible to close both throttles, lower full flap and land ahead but when the airfield boundary has been crossed the situation must be treated as a failure on a single-engine aircraft and a landing made in the best available space within the usual 60° arc either side of aircraft heading. Because of the good acceleration and engine-out characteristics of modern twins this is a situation most likely to affect older designs where a longer time is required to attain V_2. While in these cases restricted use of the live engine may help to stretch the glide towards the forced landing area this assumes that when power failure occurs sufficient height has been gained for a descending powered approach on one engine. However a modern light twin will at that height have exceeded V_2 and the problem of insufficient rudder control would not apply. The deciding factor is "Will it keep straight?" If so, gain speed, and climb away. If not, treat the situation as a forced landing.

Failure of an Engine After V_2

The importance of attaining V_2 as soon as possible during the take-off has already been mentioned. However, assuming the take-off has progressed through V_1, V_r, lift-off, then V_2 after which an engine fails, the procedure listed on page 44 should be enacted without haste but also without delay. Haste breeds fumbles. Delay can cause danger. What is required is a balance between speed and accuracy of action. Provided direction is maintained and the airspeed is kept above V_2 there is no immediate danger. The airspeed must be maintained even when lowering the nose entails a slight loss of height. Drag must be reduced without delay and it requires only a few seconds to raise the landing gear and flaps, *then* identify the failed engine and feather. Having done this the main problem is over and there should now be little difficulty in flying around the pattern.

Naturally the rate of climb will be low, particularly when fully loaded, and it is very important to use the correct engine-out climbing speed. This is normally marked with a blue line on the ASI. It should not be necessary to use maximum rpm and full throttle to climb on the live engine but be prepared to do so if the aircraft refuses to attain a safe pattern height, reducing power at the first opportunity. Remember that all your eggs are now in one basket and the instruments for the live engine should be checked, particularly during the climb.

The engine-out landing is dealt with in Chapter 6, but it is perhaps appropriate to end this chapter by reminding the reader that like most others the emergencies just described are best ensured against by regular practice. In this case practice will be of greater value when accompanied by a competent check pilot or flying instructor. Those private pilots who consider such check rides a reflection on their ability would do well to remember that professionals, civil and military, do this all the time. Or would you rather join John, wheels up on the golf course!

CHAPTER 5

Engine Failure in Cruising Flight (Multi-engine Aircraft)

PART I. THE SITUATION

Peter was quite an old hand really. Although there had been a gap in his flying between leaving Bomber Command at the end of the war and joining the flying club he never lost touch with aviation. He would read his flying magazines from cover to cover and occasionally meet up with an old squadron friend who had become an airline pilot. One way or another Peter managed to convince himself that he was still a pilot and the illusion became stronger when the licensing department granted him a Private Pilot License more or less for the asking.

Business was booming for Peter and although from time to time he went through periods of wanting to buy a company aircraft, always the idea faded when he did the sums—there really wasn't enough work to justify a company plane and he could put less money to better advantage by hiring a twin whenever the urge took him into the air. The local club had a well-equipped Aztec and perhaps once a month Peter would climb aboard with his family and head to Ostend or Le Touquet, or such places, for

Sunday lunch. Sitting behind the controls and thinking back to his days on Wellingtons he would tell himself "flying hasn't changed much" which of course was not strictly true; flying changes, at times very rapidly, and techniques improve as well as airplanes. It was the belief that wartime methods held good twenty-five years later which caused Peter many minutes of quite unnecessary anxiety and frightened his wife and children in the bargain. They were returning from Amsterdam to their local flying club in Essex. The weather was beautiful and it had been a splendid trip. They were over the North Sea with some thirty minutes to go before landfall when, without warning, the starboard engine quit. At first Peter couldn't believe it. "Motors just don't stop these days," he told himself, then without further ado, Wellington days submerging all other thoughts, he went through the drills of a quarter-century ago and feathered the starboard engine.

Ostend was nearer than base but there was a strong head-wind blowing off the Belgian coast so he opted for an emergency landing at Southend. Funny thing about single-engine flying over water is the odd noises one can imagine. It is so easy to believe that a plug is out or a cylinder head is loose and Peter spent the next twenty-five minutes convinced he was about to lose the other engine when in fact it was running perfectly. He was obviously worried, it showed and the atmosphere was becoming a little tense. The youngest was crying and the older girl looked white. To make matters worse, in his haste to make an early start Peter had forgotten the life jackets and he could only sit and sweat while his wife tried to calm the little girl. At least the Aztec was maintaining height nicely without the need to push the other engine which by now was sounding sweeter, perhaps because land was in sight.

Safely on the ground at Southend an engineer took off the cowlings and examined the offending engine. It looked perfect. He got in, started up and the engine went like a sewing machine. "You must like single-engine flying," he told Peter. "All you had to do was put the electric fuel pump on—the mechanical one has packed up."

Thirty minutes of anguish—for what? To this day his wife doesn't know it need never have happened.

PART II. THE PROCEDURE

PAID OFF

While flying a twin-engine aircraft in the cruise an engine fails.
Carry out the following drills—

Immediate Actions using the mnemonic—

PREVENT   yaw with rudder. If necessary assist with aileron.

ATTAIN   recommended engine-out speed.

IDENTIFY   the failed engine.

DECIDE   whether or not to feather. When there are obvious signs of mechanical failure or fire, feather without delay. If not—

OPEN   up power on the live engine to maintain height.

FIND   the cause of engine failure;

         Check—Ignition "on"
              Fuel contents
              Fuel pressure
              Electric fuel pump "on"
              Carburetor heat on or select alternate air source
              Change fuel tanks to failed engine
              Close the throttle and slowly open.

If engine will not restart—

FEATHER   and switch off the ignition, turn off the fuel and operate the idle cut-off.

Subsequent Actions using the mnemonic—

STAR

SAFEGUARD   vacuum and electrics.
TANKS   select for asymmetric flight as required.
AIRFRAME   clean-up. Windows and cowl flaps closed. Retrim.
REVISE   flight plan and inform Air Traffic Control of changed
             circumstances. Watch temperatures and pressures on
             the live engine.

PART III. BACKGROUND INFORMATION

There was a time when the engine-out performance of multi-engine aircraft could best be described as "marginal." The subsequent introduction of feathering propellers improved their performance to the point where height could be maintained under all but the most adverse conditions and, in some cases, a modest rate of climb was possible. During the Second World War aircraft were required to operate in overload conditions and consequently the improvements conferred by feathering propellers were sacrificed to the needs of the time, asymmetric performance suffered accordingly and it is hardly surprising that it became the practice to feather as soon as a power failure occurred. For example, the Dakota, with a normal maximum gross weight of 27,500 lbs., was often flown during the war at 32,000–36,000 lbs.

Following on the postwar introduction by many civil aviation authorities of very stringent airworthiness requirements for multi-engine aircraft, the engine failure procedure that caused Peter such unnecessary anguish in Part I of this chapter has now been supplanted by a different line of thinking, based upon the premise that a modern aircraft will continue to fly well after an engine has failed. Therefore, when in cruising flight there is no need to make hasty decisions and feather what may prove to be a restartable engine. Whereas an engine failure after take-off demands immediate feather action, in the cruise there is plenty of speed, height and therefore time to investigate the situation.

The Use of Mnemonics

An emergency of any kind is no time to be turning the pages of a check list and in common with most of the situations described in this book the value of drills applies to an engine failure in cruising flight. In this emergency there are quite a number of actions to be taken and these are best remembered by learning a simple mnemonic. By all means use a check list to confirm that every action has been completed but only after the situation has been brought under control from memory.

Actions to Be Taken

For convenience it has become the practice to deal with engine failure in cruising flight in two stages.

1. *Immediate Actions.* These are required to safeguard the aircraft while an attempt is made to diagnose the cause of failure and if possible, effect a remedy.

2. *Subsequent Actions.* These are taken to make the aircraft fly efficiently when the flight has to be continued with an engine feathered.

Practical Aspects of Immediate Actions

In going through these or any other emergency drills it may be of assistance to recite the appropriate mnemonic out loud, the one recommended for this stage of "engine failure in cruising flight" being

PAID OFF

These actions are listed in Part II, page 55, and while most of them are self-evident the matter of deciding whether or not to feather involves a number of considerations which should be examined.

When should feathering action be carried out immediately? Clearly when there is evidence of fire, visible loss of oil, smoke even without fire, or unusual mechanical noises. In any of these events rotation of the faulty engine must be stopped without delay. On the other hand violent misfirings could be nothing more serious than a magneto that has gone out of timing, while a quietly windmilling propeller is often some kind of fuel starvation—a fault that will be confirmed by the fuel pressure gauge.

The value of being able to recognize engine failure symptoms has already been mentioned in the chapter devoted to Forced Landing Without Power, and many of these symptoms are listed on page 6.

In a light twin the immediate actions can be completed within half a minute.

Practical Aspects of Subsequent Actions

The mnemonic recommended for this stage of the emergency drill is

STAR

While the drill associated with this mnemonic was listed in Part II, page 56, some clarification may be needed and each action is now explained in greater detail.

Safeguard vacuum and electric—this is a matter of selecting an alternative vacuum source when the only pump is on the failed engine although most aircraft these days have dual systems, either pump being capable of operating the flight panel. Some aircraft have a multi-position selector adjacent to the vacuum gauge for the purpose of reading the level of vacuum from each pump. It does not change the supply to the instruments and assuming the port engine fails the purpose of turning the selector to starboard source is only to check that vacuum pump for serviceability.

It is also the practice to fit a generator or alternator to each engine so that in the event of a power failure, electric power will continue normally. However in cases where there is only one generator and it is fitted to the failed engine, steps must be taken to reduce electrical load to a minimum before the battery is exhausted and the radios fail. Emergencies limiting the use of radio as a result of generator or electric failure are explained in Chapter 8.

Tanks—select for asymmetric flight as required. This action will depend upon fuel state at the time of failure and the distance to go before landing. When there is plenty of fuel and the nearest suitable airfield is well within range there is little point in changing from the fuel tank in use.

Should the failure occur when some considerable distance must be flown before landing then all the fuel in the aircraft may be required. Although only one engine is in use its power has been increased to maintain a reduced cruising speed and air miles per gallon will very probably be less than when cruising normally on two engines.

The ability to **crossfeed** fuel from the tanks normally supplying the dead engine to the live engine is common to all twin-engine aircraft but details of fuel system management may differ from one type to another. An emergency is no time to find out how the system works; learn how to crossfeed and be quite sure the fuel system is fully understood.

Airframe clean up. This is the time to tidy up the situation and trim out the rudder load. It is likely to become fatiguing over a lengthy period.

Drag must be kept to a minimum and while in some aircraft there is little the pilot can do to influence drag, these are the areas worthy of attention—

Windows should be closed.

Flaps and *landing gear* should be fully retracted and their position carefully checked.

Cowl Flaps or *vents* should be closed unless there is a danger of overheating the live engine.

Trim to fly "hands off" and so ensure accurate flying.

Revise the flight plan. While ATC will render every assistance they can only do so if they have been informed of the situation.

Even when the destination is the nearest suitable airfield it may be necessary to revise the flight plan because the loss of an engine will entail a drastic reduction in ceiling. Unless it is lightly loaded any attempt to hold the aircraft at a cruising level above its single-engine ceiling will entail operating the live engine at an rpm/throttle setting higher than recommended maximum continuous power. There can be little point in jeopardizing the live engine and an attempt should be made to route around high ground when this has to be crossed in order to reach the selected airfield.

Factors affecting single-engine ceiling are—

(a) *Gross Weight.* In an emergency entailing the crossing of high ground it may be possible to jettison removable and unnecessary load although the problem here may be controlling the aircraft while the open door disturbs the airflow over the tail. Closing it afterwards may prove very difficult since with some aircraft the door tends to remain open several inches and a sideslip towards it will very likely be necessary. It is as well to obtain advice on the particular aircraft type.

(b) *Outside Air Temperature.* Conditions known as "hot and high" are well-known detractors of take-off performance, a high altitude being associated with decreased air density. When this is compounded by a high temperature the still further reduced air density can seriously diminish the lifting power of the wing. So it is in other phases of flight, and a 10° C increase in outside air temperature will have a similar effect on ceiling performance to a 3 per cent increase in gross weight, i.e. the equivalent of another passenger in a 5,000 lb. light twin.

Nevertheless difficulties (a) and (b) should be put in perspective since the engine-out cruise performance of most modern aircraft is excellent and problems with single-engine ceiling will only occur under conditions of "hot and high." This is not intended to imply that there is no need for caution. Even when the emergency has occurred, say, over the flat areas of Holland it is important to make regular checks of the live engine instruments. While two engine failures would, under normal circumstances, be an unusual and unhappy coincidence, good fortune need not be left entirely to luck and a cylinder-head temperature raising above normal limits accompanied by a decreasing oil pressure is a sure warning that too much is being taken out of the live engine. Power should be reduced even when this means descending to a lower flight level. Alternatively it may be possible to maintain the existing altitude at a reduced power setting by using a slightly lower single-engine cruising speed.

Notwithstanding the foregoing which refers to a situation where the live engine is exhibiting signs of strain, the aim should be to make full use of the available fuel by flying at the recommended weak mixture engine-out cruise. In this way maximum range for asymmetric flight will be achieved.

Engine failure can at no time be regarded as a pleasant experience but if the recommendations of this chapter are learned, practiced at intervals and fully understood, at least the situation, should it ever occur, will be handled with a minimum of anxiety. After all, who wants to emulate Peter in this day and age?

CHAPTER 6

Asymmetric Landing and Overshoot Procedure

PART I. THE SITUATION

Harry had always displayed a tendency towards overconfidence. There was a long list of bent cars to his credit and while friends could not but marvel that he was still alive, his nearest and dearest had good reason to fear for him when he took up flying. Yet strangely enough the demanding nature of the art seemed to bring out the best in Harry and while he did not exactly treat flying with appropriate respect, at least there was no exhibitionism of the kind that had made him the most unwanted name in automobile insurance.

They say the most dangerous times in any pilot's life occur at three hours solo, three hundred hours and three thousand. For Harry trouble arrived at around the three-hundred mark. He had done a good twin conversion course with a responsible flying school and all seemed well until the day when the old over-confident Harry awoke from uneasy slumber while he was practicing asymmetric landings at the local airfield.

The instructor had warned him not to feather engines below 3,000 ft. unless there was a real emergency and he knew all about "zero thrust" procedures which were meant to simulate a feathered engine without risk. But simulation was not good enough for Harry. After all had he not seen those demonstration pilots at air displays, flying past the crowd as an engine came to a halt, followed by a zoom up, almost as though full power was on? "If they can do it so can I," he told himself, conveniently forgetting that he was a very average part-time pilot with barely 300 hrs. while "they" were exceptionally skilled with five thousand or more logged on umpteen types. And "they" were doing it all the time.

The idea was to feather an engine on the downwind leg and pull off a perfect landing opposite the club where members were sitting out in the sun having tea. And just in case anyone missed the brilliance of his performance he was going to stop the engine nearest the club which meant feathering the port one. This was fine because the more knowlegeable members would realize that this was the critical engine and he would be recognized for what he was, the club ace. No doubt Harry would have pulled it off but overconfidence cannot disguise a lack of ability or the fact that he had forgotten one important thing. The only hydraulic pump happened to be on the port engine, the one he had just feathered.

It wasn't until the Tower called him on finals and said "check three greens" that he realized the wheels were not locked down. Confidence a little strained he pulled out the hand pump, gave it a few strokes expecting the wheel lights to come up immediately. When they didn't oblige he began to panic. Although decision height had come and gone he elected to overshoot on the live engine. It was one of those often quoted moments that sorts the men out from the boys. Actually it all should have been easy because the landing gear and flaps were up and the port engine was feathered but at this point Harry pushed his luck just a little too far— he decided to unfeather the port engine and try a restart. Of course in his frame of mind and with only six hours on the type it was the worst thing he could have done because while Harry fiddled with the switches and levers up shot the nose and down slid the airspeed. Harry's private Farnborough ended more spectacularly than it began. There was a spiral descent behind the club and when the members got to the crash most of the bits were up in the trees with Harry. Fortunately there was no fire but the only recognizable part of the airplane was the rudder bar.

He is out of the hospital now and progressing so well that his nearest and dearest are determined to persuade him that flying is for the birds.

Aviation's loss will be aviation's relief.

PART II. THE PROCEDURE

Asymmetric Landing

Following an engine failure the aircraft is on the downwind leg, the propeller is feathered and the post feathering actions have been completed. Proceed with the landing as follows—

1. Plan a normal pattern.

2. When on the downwind leg complete the usual prelanding check list: BLMPF.

   Brakes off.

   Landing gear down and locked.

   Mixture rich and check for ice using carburetor heat (live engine).

   Pitch fine or as recommended (live engine).

   Fuel and electric pump on (live engine) and sufficient fuel for an overshoot.

3. Check temperatures and pressures on the live engine.

4. Turn onto the base leg and plan a rather steeper than usual engine-assisted approach, then reduce speed, lower half flap and retrim.

   Avoid losing too much height at this stage.

5. Turn onto the approach and continue the descent at a slightly higher than normal airspeed. Control the rate of descent on the live engine by watching the appearance of the runway in the usual way.

6. Correct for drift.

7. Continue the approach until decision height has been reached. If the situation looks good lower full flap, then cross the airfield boundary gradually reducing airspeed and the power on the live engine.

8. Land in the normal way. Be prepared for a tendency to swing towards the live engine as the throttle is closed.

9. If unable to taxi on one engine wait for assistance rather than risk damage to the aircraft.

The Asymmetric Overshoot

The aircraft is on finals with the failed engine feathered. The landing gear is down and locked and half flap has been lowered. Shortly before decision height it seems clear that the approach has been misjudged and the aircraft is too high for a landing.

Carry out the following procedures—

1. Check that the airspeed is above V_{mcl} and if necessary lower the nose to attain it.

2. Apply full power on the live engine. Keep straight with the rudder and if necessary assist with aileron.

3. Raise the landing gear.

4. Raise the flaps in stages, checking the airspeed and adjusting the trim control. Continue the process until the flaps are up.

5. Concentrate on maintaining a safe airspeed even if this entails some loss of height in the initial stages.

6. When the landing gear and flaps are up, adopt the correct asymmetric climbing speed. Reduce power slightly if the single-engine climb performance allows.

7. At the correct height level off, complete the pattern and try another landing.

PART III. BACKGROUND INFORMATION

Many of the considerations explained in the previous asymmetric exercises are applicable to the landing. Provided these are understood and certain precautions are taken, landing with an inoperative engine does not these days present much of a challenge. However, like any other skill there are certain "tricks of the trade" applicable to asymmetric landings which can make the procedure safer and easier to accomplish with complete success.

Rudder Trim

When an engine fails in cruising flight it is part of the subsequent actions (STAR) to trim out the rudder loads and while this certainly relieves the pilot of fatigue it should be remembered that the amount of rudder trim required will alter as the power of the live engine is adjusted. Taking the case of port engine failure, right rudder trim would have to be applied to hold on right rudder against the asymmetric power of the starboard engine. Remove the power, for example during the landing, and the rudder will take over, the result being a swing to the right. It is of course within the capabilities of the pilot to control the swing but when the type is known to possess a somewhat heavy rudder it may be preferable to wind off at least part of the trim before landing. An ideal time to do this would be on the approach while some power is on the live engine. The advantages are—

(a) Swing towards the live engine during a landing will be less after the throttle is closed than will full rudder trim, and

(b) Should an overshoot be necessary at least part rudder trim will be available to help maintain direction. The remainder can be wound on as the aircraft is cleaned up for the climb. The use of rudder trim is a matter of personal choice which can only be found during practice. Some pilots prefer the method suggested while others believe in returning the rudder trim to neutral.

Downwind Checks

The good asymmetric performance of modern light twins has often been mentioned in these pages but there may be a combination of circumstances (e.g. hot and high airfield, fully loaded aircraft, etc.) which make it advisable to delay lowering the landing gear until just before turning onto the base leg. In these cases it is preferable to delay the entire downwind check rather than recite BLMPF in the usual position and say, "Landing gear—better leave that until later" because later it may be forgotten.

When the aircraft has a hydraulic retracting landing gear and hydraulic flaps, be quite sure that the pump is in fact on the live engine. If there are two pumps then obviously the problem does not arise but guard against the situation that faced Harry in Part I and if the hand pump must be used, keep pumping until the green landing gear lights appear. And of course remember to select wheels down before using the pump. Obvious as this advice may seem there have been cases where a pilot under stress has expected the handpump to lower the flaps or landing gear without first making the correct selection.

While it used to be universal practice to move the pitch control to "fully fine" on the downwind leg, with some types of aircraft a figure is recommended, usually 2,400 rpm, and the operating manual should be consulted if in any doubt.

Planning the Approach

Avoid losing too much height on the base leg. It is better to aim for a slightly steeper glide path using moderate power on the live engine rather than attempt a normal engine-assisted approach with high asymmetric power.

The Importance of V_{mcl}

An aircraft on a normal approach will eventually be in the landing configuration, i.e. landing gear down, flaps fully down and propellers in fine or recommended pitch. Should at this stage the critical engine fail and for some reason the pilot have to initiate an overshoot with full power on the live engine the lowest speed at which he can maintain direction is known as **minimum control speed, landing configuration** or V_{mcl}. In the case of an asymmetric landing when the engine failure has occurred perhaps before joining the pattern, feather action will have been completed so that to this extent the overshoot situation (should the need arise) is better than the conditions laid down for V_{mcl} because the dead engine is not causing windmilling drag. However the possibility of having to overshoot must always be borne in mind. There could be various reasons for doing this. The approach could be misjudged; some one could taxi onto the runaway during short finals; bad weather may cause a "missed approach." Therefore at all times on the approach the airspeed must be kept above V_{mcl}, the value of which will be found in the operating manual.

Decision Height

In the event of an asymmetric overshoot the drill listed on page 65 may entail some loss of height during the transition from powered descent to asymmetric climb. It is of the greatest importance that direction is maintained during the application of full power on the live engine and with some types of aircraft this will call for a determined effort. Like all asymmetric flying the success of the exercise

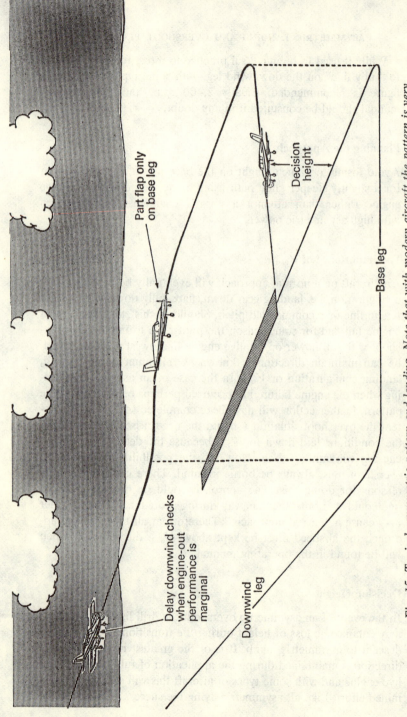

Fig. 15. *Typical asymmetric pattern and landing. Note that with modern aircraft the pattern is very similar to one flown under normal conditions with both engines functioning.*

Delay downwind checks when engine-out performance is marginal

Part flap only on base leg

Decision height

Downwind leg

Base leg

is dependent upon maintaining sufficient airflow over the rudder but during an overshoot with the landing gear down and part flap lowered much of the available power will be absorbed in overcoming drag. It may therefore be necessary to lower the nose in order to maintain airspeed during the transitional period and the extent of any height loss incurred will vary from type to type. To cater for this height loss a **decision height** is usually recommended below which an overshoot should not be attempted.

It is good practice to delay lowering full flap until decision height has been reached (usually in the region of 300–500 ft. for most light twin-engined aircraft) and there is no doubt that a satisfactory landing is possible. When the flaps are particularly effective in the drag phase it may be advisable to further delay full application until the airfield boundary is being crossed. By limiting the amount of flap until after decision height the added difficulty of contending with maximum drag will be avoided in the event of an overshoot. The asymmetric circuit, approach and landing is illustrated in Fig. 15.

The Asymmetric Overshoot

The principal aims when overshooting with a failed engine are—
    (a) maintenance of airspeed to assure—
    (b) maintenance of direction;
    (c) reduction of drag to allow—
    (d) climb to circuit height.
Requirements (a) and (b) have been discussed at some length in the previous chapters but item (c) will perhaps require further explanation.

Reducing Drag for the Overshoot

The areas under the control of the pilot are—
    Landing gear—which may be raised immediately.
    The Flaps—which should be raised in stages to avoid large changes of trim. Trim may be adjusted after each lift of flap, particular care being exercised during the last 15°–20° when an appreciable sink may occur. Some aircraft have a design feature limiting the rate of retraction and in these cases the flaps may be raised in one movement.

Windmilling Propeller

When feathering action has been completed an asymmetric over-shoot will present little difficulty provided it is started at or before decision height. On the other hand an overshoot following the sudden failure of an engine and the resulting introduction of asymmetric drag will call for immediate feathering action as a pri-ority. A windmilling propeller not only adds to total drag, it also contributes to the yaw. When the aircraft has been cleaned up and settled into the climb at the correct engine-out speed the live motor should be throttled back as soon as possible and its instru-ments checked to ensure that it is operating within pressure and temperature limits.

Practicing the Asymmetric Landing and Overshoot

After reading the story of Harry and his feathered landing the reader could be excused for not feeling encouraged to practice this emergency. But it can be practiced in complete safety by using the **zero thrust** technique. Briefly the thought behind zero thrust is that while practice flying an engine failure may be reproduced by closing a throttle. Feathering may then be simulated by opening the throttle again to the point where the engine is providing nei-ther drag nor thrust, hence the term "zero thrust." The correct throttle setting for zero thrust is quoted in the operating manual but an average figure for most light twins would be 11 to 12 in. manifold pressure. Zero thrust procedure has the advantage that, since feathering is only simulated, the throttled back engine is available for use should for any reason the asymmetric exercise become out of hand. Furthermore in providing safety, realism is not sacrificed in any way, therefore during training, pilots are strongly advised to limit actual feathering to flights at above 3,000 ft. For asymmetric exercises around the pattern use zero thrust, That is unless you wish to join Harry—in the trees.

CHAPTER 7

Fire in the Air

PART I. THE SITUATION

Flying is littered with milestones, the first solo, the first thousand hours and scores of other firsts. Naturally the issue of a Private Pilot's License is a particularly important milestone for it marks the culmination of hours spent learning a new skill in unfamiliar surroundings, to say nothing of all the necessary study, some of it tedious. One of the final hurdles is the qualifying solo cross country with its two intermediate landings on the way round—and it was a warm sunny afternoon in August when Stuart embarked on his.

As he let down into the pattern at Bristol, his first landing, a glance at the fuel gauge told him that he was using rather a lot of gas for a Cessna 150. Perhaps he had misread the gauges before take-off or possibly the gauges were not working properly. Then again, it was a hot day and this was bound to increase the fuel consumption—thus he convinced himself that all was well, for there is no end to the ingenuity of the human mind when it is determined to believe what it wants to believe.

They signed his log book at Bristol, then he booked out for the next leg and clambered aboard eager to press on. Getting back into the cabin after those few moments in the fresh air he was conscious of a strong smell of gas. This Stuart dismissed as the effect of a hot day.

The engine refused to start—which was very odd because usually this one was particularly eager to awaken at the first pull of the starter. When repeated pumping of the throttle failed to produce any response Stuart tried the primer and this did the trick. A more experienced pilot would at that point have become suspicious, as from what had occurred the likely indications were that the carburetor and its accelerator pump were bone dry and therefore it needed the primer to get fuel to the engine before it would start.

Stuart opened a window to clear away the gas fumes and taxied to the holding point. Ahead of him in the line were an HS 125 and a Viscount. To his annoyance neither seemed in a hurry to take off, which was understandable because a few moments later another 125 whistled in and landed.

Check list completed, the Cessna took off and climbed out to the planned cruising altitude of 2,500 ft., then, as he leveled out, Stuart became aware that the smell of gas had given way to an ominous one of burning, which jerked him into an acute sense of alertness. Then, to confirm his worst suspicion, came a tell-tale wisp of smoke. Somewhere in the engine bay THERE WAS A FIRE! He glanced at the fire extinguisher in its clip behind the seats and asked himself how in heaven's name it could be used to good effect.

Under normal circumstances Stuart was a quick-thinking lad; now with his survival threatened on that glorious summer day he thought harder and even quicker. At the back of his mind a message kept repeating itself like a faulty gramophone record—"This is no time to admire the countryside or wish I had stayed home and washed the car." Something had to be done, and quickly! Even louder than the "faulty record" was the voice of his instructor, urgent, insistent and almost as though he were sitting beside him in the right-hand seat. "Throttle—fuel—switches—" he did it all without panic.

Stuart turned towards a large green field that was ideal in every way for a forced landing and a stream of greyish-black smoke escaped from the cowling, fortunately without any flames.

Over the hedge, a touch of brake, stop, then off with the traps and out of the cabin. The nightmare was over.

Outside the aircraft there was evidence of intense heat; the cowlings were blackened and twisted although now the situation seemed dormant, with only a little smoke to remind him of the drama of a few moments past. He got the fire extinguisher out of the cabin and discharged it into the air intake for good measure.

Several days later the now dismantled Cessna stood looking sorry for itself in the Club hangar. Very soon they discovered a leak at the union where the fuel line from the engine pump joins the carburetor. It seemed obvious that, with the engine running, fuel under pressure from the mechanical pump was soaking the engine bay with a fine spray of gas—this all tied in with the high fuel consumption and the smell of fuel, both dismissed by Stuart as "the effects of a hot day." The long wait at the holding point before taking off from Bristol would have put up the cylinder head and exhaust temperatures, and the climb out with the engine at high power spraying fuel from a leaking union was the last straw.

Stuart and his many friends at the flying club have now developed a keen sense of smell—particularly when the flavor is gas!

PART II. THE PROCEDURE

If, while in the air, there are unmistakable signs of a fire in the engine bay, take these immediate actions to contain the situation.

Single-engine Aircraft

1. Close the throttle.
2. Turn off the fuel.
3. Check that the fuel booster pump is OFF.
4. Turn off the cabin air intake or heater to prevent smoke and fumes entering the cabin.
5. When the fire stops, switch off the ignition and operate the idle cut-off.
6. Carry out a forced landing informing Air Traffic Control of the situation and your intentions.
7. If flames enter the cabin, use the cabin fire extinguisher.

Multi-engine Aircraft (without an extinguisher system)

1. Close the throttle for the affected engine.
2. Turn off the fuel supply to the affected engine.
3. Check that the relevant fuel booster pump is OFF.
4. As the engine stops running feather the propeller, then turn off the switches and operate the idle cut-off.
5. Land at the nearest airfield, or carry out a forced landing according to circumstances, informing Air Traffic Control of the situation and your intentions.

Multi-engine Aircraft (with an extinguisher system)

1. Confirm that there is a fire and not a circuit fault in the warning system. If there is evidence of a fire—
2. Close the throttle to the affected engine.
3. Turn off the fuel and the electric engine.
4. When the engine stops running feather the propeller, switch off the ignition and operate the idle cut-off.
5. Wait for engine rotation to stop, then press the extinguisher button.
6. After the fire has ceased, land at the nearest airfield or carry out a forced landing according to circumstances, informing Air Traffic Control of the situation and pilot's intentions.

PART III. BACKGROUND INFORMATION

Fire in the air must surely appear high on the list of pilot's enemies and almost since the beginning of flying, aircraft designers have devoted much thought and ingenuity to its prevention. Some of the devices used in fire protection, particularly as related to the light airplane, are explained in this section.

Aircraft fires may be classified under these sections—

fuel fires
oil and hydraulic fluids fires
electrical fires

Fuel Fires

The most obvious cause of fire was illustrated in Part I of this chapter, i.e. leakage of fuel onto a hot engine. Fuel is conveyed from tank to carburetor by a system of corrosion resisting pipes, with lengths of flexible hose in the vicinity of the engine to allow movement within its vibration damping mountings. Other than the unlikely event of a split fuel line of flexible hose the only leaks that could occur are at the union joints or the carburetor itself. Alternatively a sticking float-needle valve would allow the carburetor to flood. Without turning this book into a technical manual it is not possible to detail the various design precautions incorporated in an engine installation. Sufficient to say that it is common aeronautical engineering practice to safeguard all nuts, screws and unions with some form of locking device which effectively prevents slackening due to vibration.

Behind the engine is a fireproof bulkhead designed to prevent the spread of fire outside the engine bay. In most aircraft with a single engine the motor is installed within a few feet of the occupants and in this case the value of a fireproof bulkhead will be obvious. Less evident are the merits of containing an engine fire when the installation is on a wing. However, without a fireproof bulkhead a serious fire would most likely spread to the wing, affect the main spar and threaten the fuel tanks.

Fortunately serious fuel fires (as opposed to minor fires in the induction or exhaust manifold—which are rarely of consequence) are, due to good design and engineering, very unlikely, although should one occur the procedure outlined in Part II is intended to—

  (a) reduce the flow of slipstream through the fire by throttling back,
  (b) cut off the fuel supply to the engine bay, and
  (c) burn the fuel remaining within the engine bay as safely as possible. This is why the ignition is left on until the engine stops running.

Generally it is best to glide normally, making correctly balanced turns towards the forced landing area. This will ensure that the fire is contained within the engine bay, shielded from the fuselage or wing by the fireproof bulkhead. Only when smoke or flames threaten the cabin or a wing tank should a gentle sideslip be made to divert the danger in an appropriate direction.

Oil and Hydraulic Fluid Fires

Modern engine oil has a low flashpoint, therefore it is extremely unlikely that an oil leak will be the cause of a fire. Rather, an engine oil fire—if one occurs—will probably have resulted from a fuel fire. Such a fire will be accompanied by prolific black smoke quite unmistakable in appearance. A fire involving hydraulic fluid is equally unlikely, unless precipitated by a serious fuel fire.

Engine oil or hydraulic fluid will continue burning until the engine stops rotating and pumping the burning liquid. For this reason, when a fire is recognized to be non-gas in origin, rotation must be stopped as quickly as possible.

Whenever there has been a fire, whatever the cause, never be tempted to restart the engine. It could all happen again!

Electrical Fires

Fires caused by faulty electrical circuits or equipment are readily discernible by the pungent acrid odor which usually precedes, then accompanies, the fire. They may occur in the engine bay, wings or within the fuselage. To the extent that a faulty circuit will normally blow its protecting fuse or circuit breaker (page 87) electrical fires are very unlikely. Those that do occur may usually be detected and the circuit isolated without difficulty.

Should for any reason the origin of an electrical fire prove impossible to determine, turn off the master switch or put the GROUND/FLIGHT switch to GROUND. This will isolate the battery from the electrical circuits. When it is possible to do so, switch off the generator(s). Only when the cause of the fire has been established may the faulty circuit or equipment be isolated by the relevant circuit breaker—which is likely to be a switch since a thermal overload or fuse would have acted automatically under the circumstances. Having taken these steps the remaining services can then be brought back "on line."

Other Fires

It is an airworthiness requirement for "NO SMOKING" notices to be affixed in the cabins of all aircraft deemed unsuitable for smoking. Regrettably there are always those who cannot pass the time for more than a few moments without lighting a cigarette while others seem to derive pleasure from disregarding the advice of the airworthiness authorities or indeed the manufacturers. When smoking is prohibited there is always a very good reason. Possibly the fuel cock itself, not just the selector, is situated within a cabin that is by no means fireproof and it only requires the act of a careless smoker to ignite whatever gas vapor may have collected near the floor when a serious fire could result, which would of course have to be brought under control with the cabin fire extinguisher.

Fire Detection and Warning Systems

Warning systems are rarely fitted to civil types of light single- and twin-engine aircraft. In these cases the detection, recognition and location of a fire, whatever its type, will be a matter of common sense using type of smoke, its odor and position within the aircraft to determine the course of action. More difficult may be the task of finding the specific cause of the fire.

Larger and more comprehensively equipped multi-engine aircraft usually have a fire warning system consisting of one or more automatic flame switches and a red fire warning light prominently positioned on the instrument panel. There may also be an aural warning.

The flames switches are situated in the engine bay(s). When they are subjected to heat beyond a preset temperature an electric circuit is completed and the relevant fire warning light will appear. A note of caution is appropriate here. When a fire warning light illuminates it must not immediately be taken at face value. Electrical circuits themselves sometimes develop faults and, before action is taken to deal with a fire that may not exist, the red warning light should be confirmed by a visual check of the engine and its instruments.

EXTINGUISHER SYSTEMS

Most light aircraft have no extinguisher system as such and the fire-fighting equipment is normally confined to a hand-operated extinguisher held in position by a quick release clip and located within reach of the pilot. These extinguishers are filled with a substance that will not produce toxic fumes when discharged; nevertheless, in the confines of the cabin the contents of even a small extinguisher are hardly calculated to improve the atmosphere and a window or the fresh air vents should be opened as soon as it is safe to do so.

With fire in the air—a rare aviation hazard—it is all too easy for pilots to take for granted the cabin extinguisher, yet, like all equipment, they require maintenance.

With some types the condition of the extinguisher is indicated by a pressure gauge and a typical example is illustrated in Fig. 16.

When dealing with a cabin fire caused by an electrical failure switch off the power supply first, then operate the extinguisher trying, if possible, to avoid other equipment known to be in working order.

When a fire warning system is fitted to an aircraft there will also be an extinguisher system in the engine bay(s). This is comprised of a cylinder containing extinguisher fluid (usually methylbromide) which is arranged to discharge through a number of nozzles directed at vulnerable parts of the engine.

Sometimes the system is of the "two-shot" type allowing the pilot two attempts at bringing the engine fire under control.

The system is activated by—

(a) Extinguisher
A safety cover is provided to prevent accidental operation of the system.

(b) An inertia switch that will operate on severe impact and activate the spray system even if the pilot is prevented through injury from taking appropriate action.

OPERATING THE FIRE EXTINGUISHER SYSTEM

While the procedure laid down in Part II for aircraft equipped with an extinguisher system is self-explanatory it will be noted

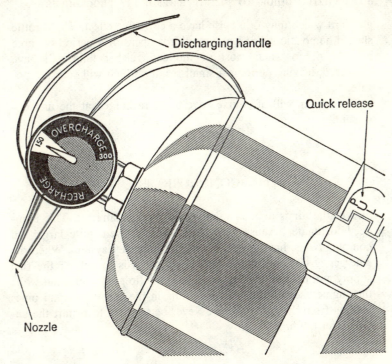

Fig. 16. Fire extinguisher in its quick release clip. Some types have an indicator pin instead of the pressure gauge.

that the extinguisher button should not be pressed until the engine ceases to rotate and the ignition is switched off. This is to ensure that most of the fuel is burned within the engine, that the exhaust system is clear of unburned gases and that there is no slipstream to assist the airflow which has a tendency to disperse the extinguishant and reduce its effectiveness. Furthermore, discharging the extinguisher into an engine in process of shutting down is likely to fill the cylinders, induction and exhaust systems with extinguishant, and it will then be necessary to strip the engine.

ACTION TO BE TAKEN AFTER ACCIDENTAL OPERATION

Should the fire-extinguisher button be pressed inadvertently while in any phase of flight the aim must be to rid the engine of extinguishant which may otherwise have a corrosive effect. The throttle should be positioned at least two-thirds open for a period of three minutes or so when most of the extinguisher fluid will have dispersed, leaving perhaps a small residue which will soon evaporate.

The system will of course have to be recharged at the first opportunity.

CONCLUSIONS

Fire in the air is almost unknown in modern aircraft. This is indeed fortunate because most light aircraft, even quite large and complex twins, have no engine-bay extinguisher system. When the emergency does occur the aim in all cases is to cut off the fuel supply and contain the fire in front of the fireproof bulkhead while the engine uses up the fuel remaining in the carburetor and pipes leading from the fuel selector. Never be tempted to restart the engine after the fire is out.

CHAPTER 8

Loss of Electrical Power and Radio Failure

PART I. THE SITUATION

Some of Geoffrey's most creative moments came when he was in the bath. So it was, one evening after a tiring day to Paris and back by schedule airline, when he lay back in the soap and bath-salts turning a rosy pink as he did some mental arithmetic. And gradually he came to a surprising conclusion. His not very exciting 120 mph light plane could get him to his business appointments on the Continent more quickly and conveniently than the jets of any large airline. There would be no getting to a major airport and that time-wasting hanging around after check in—just a quick drive to the local airfield (which happily enough had customs facilities), then a flight to one of the many airports so conveniently situated all over the Common Market, where Geoffrey was paving the way for his company in anticipation of Britain's entry. It was an attractive idea and he lost no time proving his arithmetic. Very soon he was making regular use of his aircraft which hitherto he had regarded as no more than an expensive toy.

Late one afternoon in September, after a particularly demanding day and tough bargaining, Geoffrey took off from an airfield near Paris and headed for his home airfield in the Midlands where he expected to land before dark. Over the Channel the evening sun made a splendid sight as he relaxed in the cozy cabin and congratulated himself on a good job well done. He passed his next ETA over the radio. There was no reply. Repeated calls brought no response. He changed frequency several times but the radio was dead. For the first time he noticed the OFF flag on his VOR. By now he was near the coast and a change to the Number 2 set brought no better results. It was all very puzzling.

Fortunately the ADF was working, so although Ashford Airport lay basking in the September sun he decided to press on home for a dinner date. It was a silly thing to have done. An hour later the light was beginning to fade, while factory smoke mixed with the moist air to form areas of industrial haze and Geoffrey began to wish he had landed at Ashford; but it was too late for that now. He decided to home on the "Golf Mike" beacon at Birmingham for although he was not expected there this was, after all, an emergency and they could hardly expect him to fly on another twenty minutes or so to his home base when a big well-equipped airport was so conveniently to hand. The visibility might come down and besides, they could easily send a car to pick him up at Birmingham. It could have him home in time for that dinner party.

Through drifting haze the airport beacon flashed invitingly as the ADF needle swung around. Then came the lead-in lights brightening in the growing dusk and full flap, in for a landing—home and dry.

A safe landing following an emergency, however minor it may be, always brings a feeling of elation—but for Geoffrey elation was short-lived. Birmingham Airport was not pleased to see him. Did he realize that two aircraft had been diverted, two were in the hold and in fact there hadn't been a departure for some considerable time, all because an unidentified blip on the radar screen had mysteriously appeared—his blip? Did he not know about controlled airspace? Did he not realize that Birmingham had scheduled traffic to handle? And even if his radio had failed was he not aware of the correct procedure to adopt in the event of radio failure? The matter would be reported and the possibility of a prosecution was mentioned. It was all very unpleasant for Geoffrey, a fair-minded chap who was more upset about the chaos he had caused than the possibility of having to pay a fine.

The following day a careful examination revealed that the second

NAV/COM set had been serviced but not tested and, for some reason no one could determine, the circuit breaker for Number 1 set had popped. It simply needed resetting—a little push with the finger—no more than that! The engineers were at fault for not having fixed the Number 2 set. Geoffrey was at fault for not trying it while taxiing out for Paris that morning and he was also very remiss for not having checked the fuses when his Number 1 set went off. A lot of people had been put to a great deal of inconvenience and it could have been much more serious. All because he didn't understand the electric circuit of his aircraft or "Action in the Event of Radio Failure."

PART II. THE PROCEDURE

Loss of Radio Navigational Equipment

Although radio communications are unaffected the navigation set is seen to be inoperative. Take the following actions.

1. Check the NAV set on other frequencies and if nothing can be received—

2. Check the fuse/circuit breaker protecting the equipment and if necessary reset. If the failure cannot be rectified and there is no alternative NAV receiver in the aircraft, continue the flight in accordance with one of the following procedures.

OUTSIDE CONTROLLED AIRSPACE

1. Keep clear of all controlled airspace.

2. In VFR complete the flight by map reading.

3. In IFR call the FIR controller who will arrange assistance if this is required.

IN CONTROLLED AIRSPACE

1. Call the ATC unit which may—
   (a) authorize continuance of the flight in controlled airspace, or

(b) instruct the pilot to leave controlled airspace and proceed to an airfield situated away from dense traffic, or

(c) give radar assistance if this is required and help the pilot to descend safely through cloud in preparation for a landing.

2. When the radio failure occurs in an area not covered by surveillance radar, pilots should make use of such DF facilities as are available.

3. Before letting down the IFR terrain clearance must be carefully checked.

Loss of Radio Communications (radio navigational equipment functioning)

1. Check the COM set on other frequencies and if nothing can be heard,

2. Check the fuse/circuit breaker protecting the COM set. If the fault cannot be rectified and there is no alternative COM set carry out the following procedures.

IN VFR

1. Maintain VFR.
2. Keep out of controlled airspace.
3. Land as soon as possible.
4. Immediately advise ATC of the circumstances.

IN IFR (IN CONTROLLED AIRSPACE)

1. Maintain the flight in accordance with the flight plan.
2. Maintain the last flight level (or altitude) given and acknowledged.
3. Fly to the terminal airfield radio facility at which a descent and runway approach will be made.
4. Descend in the holding pattern at not less than 500 ft. per minute.
5. Where a transponder is fitted select Mode Alpha 7600 and transponder to "ON" (*not* standby).
6. Where the destination airfield is in proximity to a VOR bea-

con transmitting ATIS (Automatic Terminal Information Service) this should be selected, because airfield information can be passed through this medium.

7. Make a standard instrument approach and landing within 30 min. of the time the descent would normally have commenced (from ETA or EAT if one had previously been given by ATC). If this is impossible but the pilot is able to complete the approach and landing visually he is permitted to do so; if not

(a) fly to an area in which flight and subsequent landing may be continued in VFR, or

(b) select an area in which to descend through cloud and then fly visually to airfield. The weather situation and terminal and area forecasts obtained from Weather Advisory Service before departure will be important information on which a decision to divert would be based; other considerations would include safety heights and fuel available.

(c) After landing advise ATC.

IN IFR (OUTSIDE CONTROLLED AIRSPACE)

1. Make the usual check of fuses/circuit breakers and try to reinstate the radio.

2. If the fault cannot be rectified fly towards an area where it is safe to let down through cloud or where VFR is known to exist.

3. Keep out of controlled airspace.

RADIO FAILURE AFTER TAKE-OFF FROM AN AIRFIELD WITHIN A CONTROL ZONE

When the aircraft has been cleared to leave the airfield frequency and communicate with ATC, a pilot experiencing radio failure should carry out the procedure listed under the heading "In VFR" or "In IFR" (page 84) according to the weather at the time.

When radio failure has occurred while still in communication with the airfield of departure observe the following procedure.

1. Maintain visual contact and land at the airfield of departure, keeping a good lookout for other traffic.

2. When weather conditions prevent the maintenance of visual

contact with the ground and there are no suitable radio landing aids, fly out of the Control Zone using standard routings (when applicable) or in accordance with the air traffic control clearance, then—

(a) check the latest weather situation,
(b) check terrain clearance,
(c) fly out of controlled airspace and aim for an area where the flight may be continued in VFR, and
(d) if necessary select a suitable area to descend through cloud and continue the flight visually to a suitable airfield.

3. After landing immediately advise the ATC service of the circumstances.

Action to Be Taken After Complete Radio Failure

IN VFR

When it is certain that the flight can be continued in VFR, proceed to the destination, study the signals area, then keeping a good lookout for other traffic, join the pattern in the correct manner and land.

IN IFR

1. Study the map and plan to avoid high ground or other obstacles.

2. Keep out of all controlled airspace.

3. Navigate by mental D/R and fly to an area where a let-down can be made in safety.

4. When there is widespread low cloud turn into wind after ETA over the chosen let-down area, lower optimum flap, then start a gentle powered descent at a low airspeed.

5. Determine the aircraft's position by relating ground features to the map, then fly to the nearest airfield (outside controlled airspace).

6. When shortage of fuel or deteriorating weather precludes flying to an airfield, find the best open area and carry out a Forced Landing with Power using the techniques described in Chapter 2.

PART III. BACKGROUND INFORMATION

Aircraft Electric Circuits

While a pilot is not expected to have an intimate knowledge of the electric circuits in his aircraft the management of the electric system must be understood if emergencies of the kind recounted in Part I are to be avoided. Like most branches of aeronautical engineering, electrical systems have become more complex as aircraft have developed. Even the light airplane has progressed from a simple circuit providing cockpit and navigation lights, powered by a battery that had to be recharged on the ground, to the modern electric system feeding comprehensive radio, full night flying equipment, flap and landing gear actuation and a host of other services that are listed on page 90f. of this chapter. Since a battery capable of sustaining all of these services for more than an hour or so would probably weigh almost as much as a passenger, an engine-driven generator is arranged to support the current load in flight and, at the same time, keep the battery up to a level of charge fit to start the aircraft. It is becoming the practice to use **alternators** instead of generators, the advantage being that taxiing or idling rpm produce a sufficient charge to protect the battery from current drain while running, say, lighting and radio on the ground prior to take-off or after landing. Most light-aircraft electric circuits operate at 12 volts although some of the light twin-engine aircraft have 24-volt circuits.

THE CHARGING CIRCUIT

The engine-driven generator or alternator charges the battery under the control of a **voltage regulator** and a **cut out** which disconnects the circuit when engine rpm fall to a level at which battery current would flow back to the generator/alternator. This part of the circuit is very similar to that used in the normal family car. The state of the battery is usually indicated by a voltmeter and the rate at which it is being charged or discharged is shown on the ammeter. In some aircraft a **generator warning light** will come on should for any reason the generator or alternator fail to charge.

PROTECTING THE CIRCUITS

The main battery/generator circuit (which in hydraulic terms may be regarded as the reservoir/pump) is divided at a junction box into individual circuits, each providing a particular service. Should, for example, a fault develop in one of the radio sets or perhaps an electrical instrument it is possible that a short-circuit may develop which could overheat the circuit, cause a fire and total loss of all electrical power. Such a possibility is quite unacceptable and therefore provision is made to provide each circuit with a "weak link" which will break before further damage is caused. It may take the form of—

(a) *a fuse of the cartridge type,* easily replaced in the air by unscrewing a small cap, withdrawing the burned-out capsule and replacing it with a spare, or

(b) *a circuit breaker* which will "pop out" under overload conditions and can be reset simply by pressing in again.

Although there are occasions when a fuse will rupture or a circuit breaker will open because of a temporary overload, the reason *may* be something more serious; therefore when a fuse is serving more than one item of equipment the fault must be found and if possible isolated. For example, suppose that a single fuse is protecting more than one radio set. Switch off *all* equipment on that circuit, fit a new fuse or reset the circuit breaker, then switch on *one* set at a time. If the fuse remains intact the fault was very likely due to a temporary overload, but when a particular item of equipment is found to blow the fuse it should be switched off, so allowing the other radio on that circuit to remain in use.

When the circuit breaker is protecting a vital service (e.g. flaps, landing gear) and for some reason it will not reset, the circuit breaker itself may be at fault. It may therefore be held in while operating the service—but care must be exercised since any smoke or smell of burning will indicate a serious overload. In these circumstances the circuit breaker must be released and, in the case of an electric landing gear, the emergency lowering system will have to be used.

Fuses and circuit breakers are usually (but unfortunately not always) positioned within easy reach of the pilot, each fuse being labeled with the name of the circuit it is protecting. It is part of a pilot's prestarting checks to ensure that all fuses and/or circuit breakers are in position.

BATTERY MASTER SWITCH

The current required by an electric starter is of very high amperage and the circuit linking battery and starter motor is wired in heavy-duty cable via a **solenoid** or manually operated starter switch. Instead of a fuse the circuit is protected by a **battery master switch** or on some aircraft a separate **starter isolation switch.** There may also be a "starter engaged" warning light which will come on if the starter dog fails for any reason to release itself from the starter ring. When this happens the engine must be shut down immediately; otherwise it will drive the starter motor at very high rotational speeds and very likely cause damage to both motor and gear train.

While the prime function of the master switch is to isolate the battery in the event of a major circuit fault, some aircraft are fitted with an external plug socket which may be used for the purpose of starting from an auxiliary power unit saving the aircraft's battery from the heavy current drain of starting. The external battery is also useful during maintenance when testing of the aircraft's electrical system would otherwise drain the internal battery. In these cases the master switch will be marked GROUND/FLIGHT. In the "flight" position the aircraft's battery is connected to the electric circuits in the normal way. When "Ground" is selected the aircraft's battery is disconnected and the external socket is brought into circuit.

TWIN-ENGINE AIRCRAFT

These days most light twin-engine aircraft have a generator on each engine, either of which will sustain the aircraft's electrical system. Even so care must be taken to ensure after engine failure that the remaining generator is at least covering the electric load. When a discharge is indicated on the ammeter, equipment must be switched off until the generator can at least cover the electric load.

Loss of Electric Power

From the foregoing it will be seen that in most aircraft the pilot may at any time monitor the electric systems through these facilities—

Facility	*Information Provided*
Voltmeter	Battery state of charge
Ammeter	Rate of charge or discharge
Generator warning light	Failure of the generator to charge
Starter engaged warning light	Starter stuck in mesh with engine starter ring
Fuses and circuit breakers	Temporary overload or fault in circuit indicated by fuse panel

From this equipment it should be possible to locate any failure, but a word of warning here. Not all electric faults are of an immediate nature and when, for example, no generator warning light is fitted the only indication that it is failing to support the battery will be shown on the ammeter, an instrument often neglected in the pilot's routine scan. Since complete generator failure will ultimately cause the loss of all electrical power a landing should be made without delay.

The extent of electrical dependence will vary widely from type to type but these are the services that might be affected by a blown fuse or circuit breaker—

Navigation lights
Cockpit and instrument lights
Landing/Taxiing lights
Anti-collision and strobe lights
Engine instruments
Some gyro instruments
Pitot or pressure head heater

Ice protection equipment
Fuel selector
Fuel pumps
Fuel gauges
Door and other warning lights
Radio installation
Stall warning light and buzzer
Landing gear lights and warning horn
Flap operation
Landing gear operation
Cabin heater fan
Electro-hydraulic pump for hydraulic services

When feathering and unfeathering is implemented by a separate electrically driven hydraulic pump there will be no fuse as such but overload will be safeguarded by the operating button which resembles a large circuit breaker.

While many of the electric services listed can in the event of malfunction be isolated without creating any major problems, one or two of these failures may well cause difficulties that warrant some guidance.

COCKPIT AND INSTRUMENT LIGHTS

Little need be said about failure at night of the instrument lighting other than to remind pilots of the simple but important insurance of always carrying a flashlight.

ENGINE INSTRUMENTS AND FUEL GAUGES

Taking the second item first, loss of the fuel gauges will mean that particular attention must be paid to the endurance of the aircraft. In effect, the watch must now become the fuel gauge.

Electric engine instruments that could be lost through circuit failure are the oil pressure gauge, oil temperature, cylinder head temperature, carburetor air temperature and on some aircraft, fuel pressure. Manifold pressure and oil pressure are not electric instruments and rpm indicators are either flexible-drive operated or powered by a self-contained electric circuit which is completely independent of the aircraft's electric system.

GYRO INSTRUMENTS

Usually the only instrument to be affected under this heading is the turn-and-slip indicator since the artificial horizon and the directional gyro are on smaller aircraft vacuum-operated. However, total failure of the gyro instruments will mean keeping clear of IFR and landing as soon as possible.

LANDING GEAR WARNING LIGHTS

Often these lights are of the "press-to-test" type but should all three green lights fail to appear and refuse to illuminate when tested a circuit fault may be the cause, rather than landing gear failure—which is explained in Chapter 13.

LOSS OF ELECTRIC FLAPS

When the flap circuit is lost and cannot be reset a flapless landing will have to be planned allowing for a longer deceleration after landing. Usually loss of flaps will add between five and ten knots to the approach and touchdown speeds of light aircraft. In a single-engine aircraft the main difficulty during this emergency is likely to be caused by poor forward visibility due to the higher than usual nose attitude.

LOSS OF LANDING GEAR EXTENSION

This is dealt with in Chapter 13, page 182 (Electric Systems).

ELECTRO-HYDRAULIC PUMP

All hydraulic systems cater for the possible loss of hydraulic pressure by providing a hand-operated pump which will cope with most emergencies associated with loss of the engine-driven or electro-hydraulic pumps.

Loss of Radio

This section may best be considered under two headings—

Navigational equipment
Communications equipment

LOSS OF NAVIGATIONAL EQUIPMENT

Whether or not the loss of a VOR or ADF set constitutes an emergency in the true meaning of the word will obviously depend upon the weather at the time and the availability of alternative radio navigational equipment. When the installation is confined to a single VOR receiver and the fault is other than a blown fuse the NAV volume control should be turned up and the station identified to ensure that the OFF flag has not appeared simply because that particular beacon has gone off the air. When change of frequency fails to bring in *any* station the receiver is obviously inoperative but sometimes the beacon can be heard although one of these faults exists—

(a) the LEFT/RIGHT needle fluctuates and refuses to respond to adjustments of the omni bearing selector,

(b) Intermittent appearance of the OFF flag accompanied by centering of the LEFT/RIGHT needle.

Either fault may, on occasions, be cleared by moving the frequency selector then returning it to the required setting.

When there is a second VOR or an ADF set it is unlikely that these too will be affected unless there has been a general power failure in the aircraft. However when all radio navigational equipment has been lost steps must be taken to avoid controlled airspace, the exception being when under radar or VDF guidance; then ATC may arrange to position the aircraft for a landing at a suitably equipped airport which could in fact be situated within a control zone.

ENSURING SAFETY IN IFR

One of the most common sources of potential disaster is the inexperienced pilot who flies into bad weather. Often the situation could have been avoided had the pilot acted early in advising ATC of the circumstances. Even assuming the loss of all radio navigational equipment there are sufficient ground facilities (DF and radar) to locate and guide an aircraft out of trouble. However this does not absolve a pilot from thinking for himself and it is vital to ensure adequate terrain clearance until such times as ATC have identified the aircraft and monitored its position for a safe let-down.

LOSS OF COMMUNICATIONS EQUIPMENT

For the purpose of this explanation it is assumed that only one VHF transceiver is carried in the aircraft and that one of the following faults has occurred.

1. *Receiver Working but Transmitter "Carrier-wave" Only.* Either the microphone is faulty (in which case an alternative instrument should be tried if one is available) or there is some other reason for the transmitter failing to modulate, i.e. radiation is in the form of a toneless hiss. This is a carrier wave on which speech has failed to imprint due to a fault in the transmitter. Usually a ground station hearing such an attempt transmission will reply, "Aircraft calling—you are carrier wave only." Unfortunately there is no standard civil procedure to cater for this not uncommon situation—although the RAF have for many years adopted the "speechless" method of communication.

2. *Complete Loss of Two-way Communications.* The procedure to be adopted under these circumstances while flying in controlled airspace is explained in the ICAO "Rules of the Air and Air Traffic Services" (PANS-RAC) under the heading "Emergency and Communication Failure." This forms the basis of the procedures adopted by all the major airlines, as well as the complicated instructions listed in the UK *Air Pilot.* The procedures listed in Part II of this chapter (page 83) are likewise based upon the ICAO publication. Interpreted in the broadest terms these instructions are intended to—

(a) keep aircraft without radio out of controlled airspace when they are not expected to be there,

(b) allow aircraft cleared for flight within controlled airspace to continue in safety after radio failure provided the agreed flight plan is adhered to. Indeed once a clearance to enter a control zone has been obtained this should be followed even if subsequent radio failure occurs,

(c) remove aircraft without radio communications from controlled airspace when no expected approach time has been acknowledged before the radio failure or when traffic is so heavy that "Delay not Determined" has been passed to the pilot. In effect this means that ATC are unable to say when traffic conditions will allow an approach to be made.

It may be considered that in leaving controlled airspace (item c) and flying to another airfield a pilot is exchanging one problem for another but an aircraft departing the airways or a control zone and descending in the FIR without instructions to do so is bound to attract radar attention immediately. Furthermore the ATC service will then be alerted to the emergency.

ACTION TAKEN BY ATC AFTER LOST RADIO CONTACT

When an aircraft loses radio contact in IFR and is seen on radar to be departing from the expected flight plan the ATC unit concerned will transmit "blind" to the aircraft; the pilot may be unable to answer although his receiver could be functioning perfectly. Equally the aircraft's receiver may have failed although the transmitter is operative and pilots should likewise transmit their intentions "blind" in the hope that ATC will be able to hear.

An ATC unit handling an aircraft with lost communications will transmit the following information using the frequency on which the pilot is believed to be listening as well as the voice frequency of the radio navigational aid (e.g. VOR beacon) likely to be in use by the aircraft at the time—

1. Action being taken by the ATC unit.

2. Special instructions applicable to the emergency.

3. Details of suitable let-down areas, chosen to avoid heavy traffic and/or high ground.

4. Weather conditions in the let-down area and at airports suitable for a diversion.

Other aircraft in the area will be warned of the situation as will all ATC units along the route and in the area of diversion. In view of the obvious disruption that occurs to air traffic during these measures it is particularly important that pilots of aircraft with lost radio communications should on landing advise their arrival to the ATC service without delay.

FLYING TRAINING IN CONTROLLED AIRSPACE

Some flying schools are based on airfields situated within controlled airspace. When there is a weather deterioration, training aircraft may be recalled or given an amended clearance. In the event of a radio failure the zone should not be re-entered unless there is an emergency but a landing should be made outside controlled airspace.

ESTABLISHING VISUAL CONTACT AFTER RADIO FAILURE

The seriousness or otherwise of lost radio communications is dependent upon the weather at the time and the navigation aids available. Possibly the worst case, total loss of all radio when out of sight of the ground, is one that will illustrate the importance of (a) knowing the aircraft's position at all times and (b) having a general picture of the weather situation around the intended route. For example, if it is known that, to the east, cloud cover is ⅜ at 800 ft. although the ground is completely obscured in the present location a pilot should proceed as follows.

1. Use the map to avoid controlled airspace and high ground obstructions.

2. Fly on an easterly heading and aim for a low-lying area.

3. As the cloud begins to break up, descend VFR through a suitable gap.

4. Fuel and weather permitting, land at the nearest airfield or carry out a Forced Landing with Power (Chapter 2), according to circumstances.

When unbroken low cloud is known to cover a large part of the country a descent on instruments will be unavoidable and the prime consideration must be to avoid obstructions. Ideally such a let-down should be made—

(a) into wind (low ground speed),

(b) with optimum flap, and

(c) at a powered rate of descent of 250 ft./min. or less.

If the visibility is known to be at least 1,000 yards, whenever possible such a descent is probably best made over the sea. However in conditions of very poor visibility it is often difficult to distinguish between sea and haze, and the dangers of trying to fly visually under these circumstances will need little amplification here. In very restricted visibility the let-down is better made over low-lying ground which must be chosen with care before the descent, using the map to avoid towns, power cables or other obstructions.

FLYING TO THE LET-DOWN AREA

During an emergency of this kind the watch assumes particular importance as a vital tool of DR navigation. Ground speed will have to be estimated, distance to the chosen let-down area measured and converted into flying time and an accurate heading must be steered allowing for estimated drift. To cope with the workload and relieve anxiety during what can only be described as a demanding situation, the value of accurate trim both before and during the descent cannot be overemphasized.

CONCLUSIONS

Modern radio equipment has enabled the light airplane to fly in conditions that not so many years ago would have been beyond the capabilities of some commercial aircraft, but the benefits conferred by this equipment bring with them the dangers of exceeding the capabilities of aircraft and pilot. A light airplane fitted with a single NAV/COM set is not suitable for all weather operations because when the one and only radio fails (and even the best equipment can do that) the pilot may be left in a situation that is both dangerous to himself and a hazard to other traffic.

There are no "trade secrets" to be learned if the emergencies of this chapter are to be avoided. A pilot is simply required to know his electric system and never attempt to fly in conditions beyond his own skill or the capabilities of the aircraft, and as Geoffrey will now tell you, never arrive unannounced in controlled airspace!

CHAPTER 9

Action in the Event of Enforced Change of Flight Conditions

PART I. THE SITUATION

Julie was quite a dish, tall with fair hair, blue eyes, a charming friendly manner and a fuselage guaranteed to turn the head of any discerning male. And the outstanding thing about her was that she found popularity with all the members of the local flying club, men and women alike.

Although she had a job in the Midlands most of Julie's family and close friends lived near the Scottish border so, at intervals, when the weather was good and there was a little cash to spare she would fly home for a long weekend. That Friday morning she had been up at first light, checking the weather—and from all accounts a good high-pressure system looked settled over most of the country.

On arrival at the club Julie was dismayed to learn that her favorite aircraft, a well-equipped Cessna 172 had become unserviceable with a mag drop, one that was proving rather difficult to clear but "they were working on it" and being the nice, well-adjusted girl she was, Julie took herself off for a cup of the tepid brown liquid optimistically referred to by the local club as "coffee." She read one or two back numbers of *Flight,* then her eye caught an accident report that had somehow got itself mixed up with the untidy pile of magazines. It told the story of a foolhardy one who had set out on a flight without first obtaining a weather report. And the only flight plan was a line drawn on the map. According to the report bad weather brewed up and since the tanks had not been filled before take-off the pilot only just managed to pull off his special version of a Forced Landing with Power which involved leaving the aircraft an immobile heap in the middle of the field. The pilot was all right but the aircraft never flew again.

By now Julie's intended departure was two hours behind schedule. She was about to call off the trip when the phone rang and the voice at the other end said, "We've fixed it." A good pre-flight inspection revealed nothing out of the ordinary so Julie threw her suitcase onto the back seat, tied it down with the straps, then took off into the blue. Soon she had cleared the airfield and was advising the Flight Information Regional Controller of her flight level, position and ETA Carlisle.

The first forty minutes was fine; very little wind, groundspeed pretty much the same as airspeed, heading more or less the same as track and ETA likely to be on the nail. Then approaching the Lake District hazy conditions began to develop and Julie, anxious to remain in visual contact with the ground, started to descend. A couple of severe jolts proved a little unnerving and acted as a reminder that up and down drafts are often the playmates of mountains. "Thank the Lord I tied the suitcase down," she told herself, giving an extra pull on her own seat belt for luck. There were some drops of rain on the windshield. Now that was very odd because the weatherman on duty at 6 A.M. had promised widespread skies of blue. Clearly there had been a deterioration in the weather and with haze and now cloud it became necessary to descend even further if visual contact with the ground was not to be lost. Some of the higher peaks were looking aggressively close and it was a situation that could not be allowed to continue.

Instrument flying was a pastime that had never appealed to Julie. It was a long time since she had done any but she was sensible enough to recognize the dangers of mixing it with the mountains in poor weather. If only she had taken that IFR rating but it was no time for regrets and Julie knew it. She climbed back to her cruising level with a feeling of relief that the peaks were far below. Seconds later the Cessna was being flung about, it had become rather dark and hail was lashing the windshield. For a few moments the turbulence diminished, then just as suddenly returned with renewed vigor. It was all Julie could do to control the aircraft and she later admitted that the dark and the violent bumps mixed with hail that even drowned the noise of the engine had been the most frightening experience of her twenty-eight beautiful years. Fortunately she was no fool. "I'm in the cu-nimbs" she told herself and wondered how long it would be before the wings came off or control was lost through sheer lack of skill at instrument flying. She called the Flight Information Regional Controller and told him all her troubles. A calm voice replied, telling her to climb from flight level 45 to FL 65, to check the altimeter on 1013.2 and to contact radar on 126.5. It was reassuring to hear Humbler Radar ask for a turn onto North, then confirm, "You are identified." Somehow the turbulence seemed to lessen and even the hail had a more friendly ring about it but she was still rather punch drunk from the past hectic moments. Who would have thought that a Cessna could gain 2,000 ft. in seconds without touching the throttle!

It was not long before Julie had been directed away from the worst of the turbulence and into the clear at 2,500 ft. By then Teesside Approach had taken over. What had gone wrong? How did a switched-on lass like Julie get herself in such a fix? After all, had she not prepared a flight plan and got herself a weather report? That was it—the weather report, taken over the phone at 6 A.M., some five and a half hours before take-off. If only Julie had rechecked the weather she would have known about the deterioration and could so easily have routed around it. As it was she had relied upon an *old* weather report and after becoming committed to instruments there was no real plan to deal with the situation. It had been an unnerving experience for Julie; she kept thinking of the chap in the accident report and was thankful at not having shared his misfortune. What if she had written off her beloved Cessna? It could all so easily have ended in tragedy.

PART II. THE PROCEDURE

Flying into Deteriorating Weather

An unexpected weather deterioration occurs towards the end of a journey covering several hundred miles. There is insufficient fuel to return to base so a diversion and possible radar assistance must be considered. Carry out the following actions.

1. Check seat belt for tightness.
2. Advise ATC of changed flight conditions.
3. Check minimum safe altitude and altimeter setting.
4. Synchronize the DG with the magnetic compass.
5. Check tanks and fuel endurance.
6. Check airframe and engine ice protection as applicable to the aircraft type.
7. Safeguard instrument supply (pitot heater on, etc.).
8. Switch on navigation lights and rotating beacon.
9. Follow ATC instructions.

Flying in Severe Turbulence

While flying in unstable weather conditions it becomes necessary to complete the journey through an area of cumulus clouds. Adopt the following procedures.

BEFORE ENTRY

1. Check all seat belts for tightness.
2. Secure all loose articles.
3. Disengage the auto pilot.
4. Turn up the cockpit lighting to maximum brightness.
5. Switch off all radio being affected by static interference.
6. Operate the anti-icing and de-icing equipment. Check that the pitot heater is switched on.
7. Reduce power to maintain the recommended rough-air penetration speed and retrim.
8. Check the vacuum and/or electric supply to the instruments.
9. Synchronize the directional gyro with the magnetic compass.

AFTER ENTERING CLOUD

1. With reference to the artificial horizon, concentrate on maintaining lateral and fore-and-aft level. Avoid any harsh control movements likely to add further to the airframe stresses caused by the turbulence.
2. Unless there is a risk of hitting an obstacle ignore the fluctuating readings of the altimeter and the airspeed indicator.

3. Limit all turns to small heading corrections.

4. When weather radar is fitted use it to indicate the best way through the storm; otherwise it is usually best to keep flying straight ahead.

PART III. BACKGROUND INFORMATION

THE IMPORTANCE OF FLIGHT PLANNING

If the skies always remained clear of low cloud and the visibility never dropped below five km flight planning would be confined to the simple and obvious: ensuring sufficient fuel for the journey and observing weight and balance limits. But the weather, particularly in the northern parts of Europe, cannot be guaranteed over long periods. While every care is taken in the preparation of weather forecasts, local deteriorations do occur, particularly in coastal regions and mountainous areas, having a physical effect on humidity, temperature and air movement. Then again fronts sometimes cross the country faster than expected while others fail to materialize. Cumulus or cumulonimbus clouds and their associated thunderstorms may develop on a purely local basis quite outside any expected frontal system and then there are the various forms of fog which constitute a trap for the unwary. Fortunately the unpredictable nature of the weather is to some extent mitigated by actual reports from airfields and aircraft in flight. Much up-to-date information may be obtained on the Volmet frequency and some of the VOR voice frequencies.

It is an imprudent pilot who will set out on a flight away from the local area without first obtaining a recent weather report. The word "recent" is important; it was the omission of this factor that caused Julie so much unnecessary anxiety in Part I. While flight planning is a subject that should be as well known to pilots as medium turns, investigations often reveal a remarkable degree of laxness in preflight preparation. Therefore it may be opportune to revise some of the important aspects to be considered.

1. Study the route and determine the sector safe altitudes.

2. Obtain a wind velocity for that cruising level, compute the

heading, groundspeed, elapsed time and allow sufficient fuel for a diversion and a possible hold.

3. Note the frequencies of all VOR and NDB's likely to be of use on the flight and at the terminal airfield.

4. In these days of radio navigation it is still advisable to have a topographical map prepared. Some of the newer series show the principal radio beacons. While a radio facilities chart is essential for flights in controlled airspace its value as an aid to radio navigation, even in VFR, should not be ignored.

5. A computer is useful in the air as well as before flight. It may be used for checking the groundspeed, revising the ETA, calculating fuel consumption and all the usual in-flight checks.

6. Obtain up-to-date details of the weather, not just that covering the route but over the area as a whole. This would be of value if radio communications were lost while over cloud and a letdown had to be made in more broken weather (page 96f.).

So prepared, the pilot will be able to fly his required headings, heights and on his chosen beacons, there being little more to occupy him other than routine calls to the Flight Information Regional Controller, advising him of position, flight levels and intention so that others flying in the area may be informed and safeguarded. For aircraft flying below transition altitude the controller will provide altimeter settings thus ensuring that a flight towards low pressure does not precipitate a gradual descent while following the altimeter—a very real hazard when flying in IFR over high ground.

CHECKING THE WEATHER EN ROUTE

The normal adjustments to heading and ETA together with routine fuel checks should demand little of the pilot's time, allowing him to compare the actual weather with that forecast. Gone are the days when almost every flight was a journey into the unknown and by using his radio a pilot should not at any time be left in ignorance of the weather ahead or at the point of intended landing. However during a weather deterioration a VFR flight plan presents certain problems because it is based upon the assumption that navigation will proceed in visual contact with the ground or alternatively, "VFR on top." While for the reasons already mentioned there is rarely any excuse for the weather to take any pilot by surprise, rapidly changing conditions can make it impossible to maintain visual contact. Then commitment to instruments becomes inevitable and this must entail a change in flight plan. The procedure to adopt in an enforced change of flight conditions was listed in Part II of this chapter and those actions requiring further amplification are dealt with here.

ADVISING ATC OF CHANGED FLIGHT CONDITIONS

Contrary to the belief held by some private pilots the Air Traffic Control Service is there to help, not to hinder. This help can be the difference between anxiety or even an accident resulting from poor weather, and an expertly conducted ground-monitored diversion or let-down at the intended destination.

Pilots flying in the FIR who experience a weather change that is preventing the maintenance of visual contact with the ground should without delay advise ATC, normally the Flight Information Regional Controller, of their changed circumstances. When there is a reasonable level of instrument-flying ability little difficulty should be experienced in complying with instruction passed from the ground, but a pilot with limited instrument-flying experience should make this clear to the controller. The controller will then realize that although no emergency exists assistance is required to steer the aircraft towards an area where visual flight may continue. In either case, provided all instructions are complied with, the safety of the aircraft is ensured while the risk of collision with other traffic is minimized.

THE PILOT'S RESPONSIBILITY

While a pilot in need of help may expect very considerable assistance from the Flight Information Regional Controller certain obligations remain with him as captain of the aircraft and these are included in the list on page 101. For example, an incorrect altimeter setting has often been the cause of a serious or even fatal accident. This is the pilot's responsibility, as is the maintenance of a safe altitude or flight level for the area in which he is flying.

In the stress of the moment it would be very easy to neglect the periodical synchronization of the DG with the magnetic compass. Fuel state must be checked and the correct tank selected. There is no such thing as a good time to have a tank run dry but an empty tank in poor weather could hardly be worse. Airframe and engine icing is of sufficient importance to warrant a separate chapter (Chapter 10, page 113).

SAFEGUARDING THE INSTRUMENTS

Few aircraft these days are dependent upon a venturi tube as the sole vacuum supply to the gyro instruments and it would certainly be unwise to operate such an aircraft in icing conditions. Most modern light aircraft incorporate a vacuum-operated artificial horizon and directional gyro with an electrically driven turn-and-slip indicator acting as an independent back-up reference. This safeguards the possibility of complete loss of flight instruments should the engine-driven pump fail for any reason. When the flight panel is entirely dependent upon electric drive care must be exercised to ensure that the generator(s) is maintaining sufficient charge to cover the heavy current demand which will result when most of the aircraft's equipment is called into use to cope with the weather conditions.

NON-INSTRUMENT PILOTS

It goes without saying that a pilot who is unable to fly on instruments has no right to endanger himself and others by flying in marginal weather that is almost certain to deteriorate. Such a pilot may be likened to that breed of motorist which drives down the highway in thick fog at 70 mph. The results of this irresponsible mentality are all too often in the news but if such drivers are a menace on the road there is even less room for his kind in the air. On the other hand, the pilot who has taken the trouble to practice instrument flying will know the true value of this added skill.

One of the great aids to accurate instrument flying is the ability to relax when the workload is high and instructions are being received from ATC. A carefully prepared flight plan, listing all the relevant frequencies, will do much to ease the burden and allow the pilot to concentrate on flying his aircraft.

FLYING IN HEAVY PRECIPITATION AND TURBULENCE

Although neither precipitation nor turbulence may be regarded as an emergency, extremes of either can create very real difficulties, particularly for the inexperienced pilot. It is all a question of degree. Normal conditions of unstable air or wind gusts will cause no more than discomfort, whereas flight within a large cumulus or cumulonimbus cloud could well have serious consequences were the incorrect techniques adopted. Before considering these techniques it would be well to consider afresh the nature of cumulus-type clouds.

Although a cold front of well-developed cumulus clouds may extend for several hundred miles and have a depth of up to fifty miles their formation is not confined to the lifting of moist air within a cold frontal system. Cumulus-type clouds may result from the effects of surface heating and it is not uncommon to see these towering masses growing rapidly on a hot summer's day. The larger examples will often ascend to the tropopause when, due to temperature stabilization at that level and the greatly reduced air density, further growth is confined to a spreading outwards of the cloud head which results in the characteristic "anvil" of cumulonimbus clouds. Very considerable energy is contained within these clouds; thermal currents, both ascending and descending, have been measured at speeds in excess of 4,000 ft./min. Vast quantities of moisture are carried up and down within these vertical currents, freezing in the higher regions, then collecting further layers of water lower down before rising again, the cycle being repeated until the frozen particle has become too heavy to be sustained within the cloud when it falls to the ground as hail.

Hailstones can vary in size from as small as a grain of rice to as large as a golf ball. In a large cumulonimbus cloud water is present in various forms: water vapor and rain in the lower regions, super cooled water that freezes on impact in the main body of the cloud, also hailstones, while the upper or anvil region is composed of ice crystals (Fig. 17).

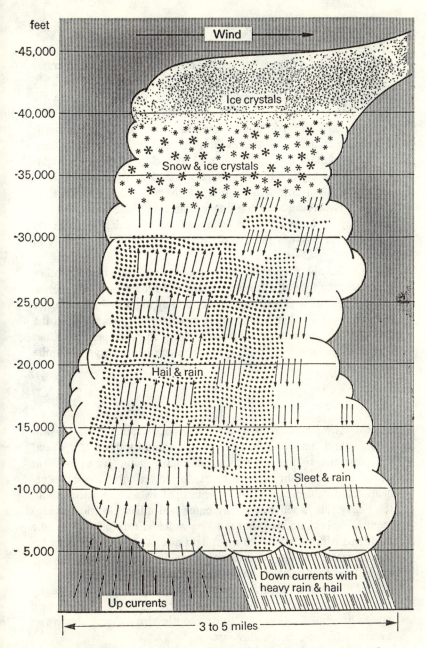

Fig. 17. Fully developed cumulonimbus cloud showing internal currents. After this stage the cloud will decline.

LIGHTNING

Friction between the vertical currents within the clouds generates static electricity when the entire cloud mass becomes increasingly charged to a very high voltage, until the resistance of the air breaks down when a discharge will occur. This takes the form of a lightning flash to earth, to another cloud or within the cloud itself. The air in contact with this flash is instantly heated to white heat and the resultant explosion is heard as a clap of thunder. Lightning is more unpleasant than dangerous and there should be little damage to an aircraft flying through a thunder storm provided the bonding is serviceable. Bonding of all components in electrical continuity is intended to prevent serious lightning damage by avoiding the risk of "flashover" from one part of the aircraft to another.

When the atmosphere is carrying a high electric charge another manifestation takes the form of St. Elmo's Fire, a brush-type electrical discharge which is most noticeable at night or in the darker regions of cloud when a blue flame or halo will appear around the propeller(s) sometimes accompanied by minute electric flashes across the windshield. Both types of electric discharge are quite harmless.

HEAVY PRECIPITATION

Rain. The problems of flying in the heavy rain associated with cumulus and cumulonimbus clouds are primarily those of reduced visibility, the risk of airframe and engine icing (dealt with in Chapter 10) and, in extreme cases, the lowering of the cylinder-head temperature. A normally watertight cabin can succumb to the heavy rain when water may enter and affect electrical equipment. This is something that must be watched carefully. While the problems will not arise with most light aircraft some of higher performance may suffer the removal of paint from the wing leading edges and other parts of the airframe unless speed is reduced.

Hail. Severe hail must be treated with respect and it is certainly advisable to reduce airspeed, particularly in parts of the world where hailstones are known to develop in size to the point where severe airframe damage may result.

Snow and Sleet. Flying through snow and sleet (a mixture of snow and rain) is primarily a matter of coping with the considerably reduced visibility but there is also the risk of impact icing and this could block the engine air intake or affect the engine temperature.

Maneuvering on the Ground. All forms of precipitation can have a marked effect on braking efficiency and this is dealt with in Chapter 13. When loose snow or slush is present on the runway, damage to the flaps has been known to occur during landing and it is probably best to limit depression to the smallest setting consistent with the available landing run, remembering again that a wet or icy runway will affect braking.

SEVERE TURBULENCE

There may be occasions when for air traffic or other reasons a line of cumulus-type clouds must be entered but, by and large, pilots would be well advised to avoid clouds of great vertical extent, certainly the developed cumulonimbus. In some parts of the world cumulonimbus may be concealed within great areas of moist but stable layer clouds; therefore without weather radar avoidance is more or less impossible. However when it is known in advance that a large cumulus or cumulonimbus cloud must be entered the procedure to adopt is shown in Part II (page 101). Many of the actions listed are no more than matters of good airmanship. The less obvious actions are—

Disengaging the Auto Pilot. Few types of auto pilot are cleared for operation in severe turbulence. They tend to add to the existing high stresses while flying in thunder clouds by trying to hold a constant height and attitude, a task better performed by human hands under these conditions.

Turning up the Cockpit Lighting. There are two reasons for doing this. It is quite dark in the larger clouds and when the cockpit lights are at maximum brightness they will prevent temporary blindness following a lightning flash.

Reducing Airspeed Before Entry. It would be unthinkable to drive a car at high speed over a badly rutted road and it could be particularly dangerous to fly at high speed through the severe turbulence of a cumulus-type cloud. The correct penetration speed, which is a balance between avoiding excessive airframe stress and keeping above stalling speed, is listed in the operating manual and is sometimes shown on the ASI as an amber arc. When the figure is not known, 1.6 times the stalling speed (clean) would be near the best penetration speed.

HANDLING TECHNIQUES AFTER ENTERING CLOUD

Until a development flight investigated the problems associated with flying in cumulonimbus clouds it was not realized that most previously known cases of aircraft disintegrating were the result of pilot overcorrection rather than the turbulence itself. Severe as it undoubtedly is, turbulence on its own will not cause structural failure, although a combination of such turbulence and the effects of overcontrolling probably will unless the aircraft is stressed for aerobatics. The procedure listed on pages 101–2 has been devised to prevent such a combination of factors by limiting all corrections to the maintenance of attitude and a more or less steady heading. On no account should attempts be made to hold a steady airspeed since this will possibly vary from near the stall to above normal maximum. There may also be large fluctuations of height and these too should be ignored provided there is no danger of flying into the ground. Experience has shown that one current has a tendency to correct another and to some extent average the aircraft's height.

No attempt should be made to fight every bump. The best technique is to "ride" the storm, use the artificial horizon as a reference and maintain a reasonable degree of pitch and lateral level. Make all corrections smoothly and fly straight ahead or, when weather radar is fitted, through the best path indicated. In the case of non-jet aircraft it has been found best to fly through the storm at a height of less than 10,000 ft. Provided there is sufficient clearance between cloud base and terrain it is possible to fly below cloud but pilots should be prepared for down-drafts.

After flying through a thunder storm the magnetic compass will almost certainly be affected and care must be exercised not to be misled by erroneous readings. The DG may be checked against a VOR radial but ADF will be of little value until the thunder storm is some distance away since the radio compass may tend to swing towards the storm area in preference to an average powered NDB.

THE TERMINAL LET-DOWN

To an instrument-rated pilot a let-down through low cloud or a landing in very reduced visibility is no more than routine. On the other hand an inexperienced pilot having to face a situation of this kind after being caught in bad weather may regard it as the emergency of a lifetime. In fact it is nothing of the kind, unless the pilot has little or no knowledge of instrument flying or the use of radio navigation equipment.

In the situation described in Part I, Julie was instructed by the FIR Controller to climb, so ensuring adequate terrain clearance and improving both radar and DF reception. The FIR Controller then transferred her to Humber Radar which gave her headings to steer for Teesside, the diversion airport. At this point the Teesside Approach Controller took over. Julie was fortunate because by then she had broken cloud and was in the clear. However while ATC will always aim to guide an inexperienced pilot towards better weather a situation could exist where even the best area would mean some kind of instrument let-down.

Assuming conditions of cloud cover down to, say, 1,000 ft. and poor visibility below, the following are the methods open to a pilot approaching an airfield after receiving guidance in bad weather.

Aircraft with Radio Navigation Equipment. When the airfield has a let-down area marked by a VOR or an NDB the pilot should fly to it after obtaining clearance, then descend at the instructed time. When ILS is available the landing can be made in conditions limited only by the ability of the pilot.

Aircraft with Communications Radio Only. When there is no radio navigation equipment or when the pilot is not qualified to use it, guidance onto the approach may take the form of DF or radar. Unless the DF let-down has been practiced it is perhaps one of the most difficult procedures for the inexperienced pilot, whereas radar entails no more than following instructions from the controller. It is also very accurate.

Whatever the method used for the terminal let-down and approach it is important that all instructions are complied with. Headings must be steered accurately, altimeter settings must be double-checked and heights must be adhered to. Unless otherwise instructed, essential information must be read back to the controller—altimeter settings, headings, frequencies, etc. When told, for example, to leave FL 40 and descend to an altitude of 3,000 ft. on the appropriate QNH the pilot should call "leaving flight level four-zero" and on arrival at the new altitude "level at three thousand on the QNH." It is important to have a knee pad or similar to write down figures passed by the controller; the QNH and QFE, headings to steer, radio frequencies, etc. This is a time when frequencies have to be changed when passing from one controller to another and an incorrect selection, confirmed by "no station" followed by the realization that the original frequency has been forgotten, is a time-wasting sequence that can only add to the already considerable work load.

While flying on instruments and listening to Air Traffic Control instructions the degree of concentration will be higher than usual but this is not an invitation to overlook the prelanding check list and so create another problem. When the airfield does appear, possibly in heavy rain, open the clear vision panel if one is fitted. Look out for cross wind and allow for drift and be prepared for the effects of wind gradient near the ground. Finally, having made a good landing after an eventful flight, remember the postlanding checks before taxiing in!

CONCLUSIONS

Most of the contents of this chapter are applicable to the pilot of limited experience who finds himself in weather conditions that demand instrument flight, possibly in heavy rain or hail and turbulence. Such conditions may place him at the limit of his ability. While the problems that accompany a weather deterioration are by no means insurmountable the chapter is intended to illustrate the need for proper flight planning, including provision for a diversion should it be necessary. The best way to avoid the kind of experience suffered by Julie is to obtain a *current* weather report, consider it, then only fly when certain that your experience and qualifications will meet the need. Remember the old saying— "Aviation is a good servant and a bad master."

CHAPTER 10

Engine and Airframe Icing

PART I. THE SITUATION

One of the snares with the light airplane is that you can fill it with radio and then convince yourself it is fit for all weather flying, which of course it is not. The ability to fly safely on instruments, obeying the indications of VOR and ADF is one thing. Coping with icing in its various forms is quite another, as the hero of this little story found out.

Ever since he took up flying after the war Ron had led something of a charmed life. There was the low-flying affair when his tailwheel caught some minor power lines and plunged a small village into total darkness (the law never caught up with him either!), the forced landing in thick fog when he found a disused airfield sitting under the only clear patch of sky for hundreds of miles around—and the time he visited a farmer friend, landed in a field so small that they had to dismantle the plane and take it home by road. People used to say that if ever the day came when Ron suffered engine failure above cloud while crossing the Channel, waiting for him below would be an aircraft carrier.

The touring addicts of Ron's favorite club had spent a well-wined-and-dined weekend as guests of a leading French school of flying and the time had come to depart. At the little grass airfield set in the green fields of Normandie long faces stared at the low scudding clouds and thin penetrating rain, studied the weather report and decided it was not on, for the time being at any rate. The danger of this kind of situation is always the overconfident member who must get back in time for a business appointment. Not only is he prepared to gamble his own neck but the inexperienced and weak-minded are prone to follow his example. To be fair, Ron was a very competent pilot but he was inclined to lean heavily on his traditional luck. Naturally, he had to be the one with the pressing business appointment but at least he was responsible enough to advise his fellow club members not to risk the weather but to wait for an improvement while he pressed on home in the club Jodel.

The others watched with mixed feelings of admiration and anxiety as the Jodel took off then disappeared in and out of low cloud at five hundred feet. Ron flew up the French coast to Cap Gris Nez before heading along the light airplane corridor and across the narrowest part of the Channel. The VOR was working perfectly and at intervals he could see below as a gap in the clouds flashed by. Periodically he would check his engine instruments and open the throttle a little to restore engine revs. In retrospect it seems strange that he was not alerted by this persistent need to open the throttle.

He called Ashford Airport giving his flight conditions and ETA. They told him to climb immediately to 1,000 ft. Now he was in it, good and thick.

It was shortly afterwards that Ron became aware of a slight roughness in the engine and for the first time it registered that the throttle was almost fully open although if anything the engine rpm were rather less than usual for normal cruise. The roughness was becoming more pronounced and soon the rpm began dropping at an alarming rate. He tried the switches and they made no difference. He turned on the electric fuel pump and changed tanks but that did nothing either. Then it dawned on him, something he had often read about but for some inexplicable reason had never before experienced. "Carburetor Icing" had been screaming at him and at last he had got the message. He pulled out the heat control and the engine began to splutter, the revs went off the clock and it sounded like a bag of nails. This apparent change for the worse seemed to convince him that perhaps it was not carburetor icing after all. Perhaps the trouble was mechanical or even dirt in the fuel. Hastily pushing in the heat control Ron called Ashford on the radio and told them his engine was failing. He started a gentle descent and as the Jodel broke cloud at 500 ft. the engine died a rather final death. There in the distance was Ashford Airport, in the clear and unattainable. Below was a large green field. It was Ron's luck again!

Next morning an instructor from the club drove to the field with one of the mechanics. They inspected the aircraft and found nothing out of place so the pilot got in, primed the engine, put on the switches and pulled the starter. She fired immediately and ran like the often quoted sewing machine. It was a big field and a nice day so they flew the Jodel home.

There is of course no mystery surrounding this incident. Quite simply Ron had been caught off guard. The weather was bad, he was glued to his instruments and being convinced that carburetor icing could not happen at cruising power he *failed to recognize the abnormal*—something this book is all about. Certainly he had experienced carburetor icing but having ignored the warnings Ron allowed it to develop. The result: a persistent loss of power, gradual at first, followed by rough running which so often indicates a substantial build-up of ice and the onset of a rich mixture cut, precisely what happened to Ron. At this stage application of carburetor heat started to melt things, sending ice and water where ice and water should not be, never calculated to improve the sweet temper of an engine.

If Ron had only persisted with carburetor heat it is almost certain the engine would have cleared. Now he knows.

PART II. THE PROCEDURE

There is a progressive loss of power followed by rough running indicating carburetor icing. Clear the engine by carrying out the following procedure.

1. Leave the throttle in its present position.

2. Apply full carburetor heat and be prepared for a further power loss accompanied by still rougher running.

3. If carburetor icing persists increase the engine temperature by—

    (a) gently opening the throttle to maximum power, taking care not to stall the engine,

    (b) climbing to reduce the cooling airflow and

    (c) lean the mixture—but guard against causing it to cut—it may then be difficult to restart.

4. Keep out of cloud and rain if at all possible.

5. When the engine is running normally return to level flight, adjust the mixture and select cold air. Check that the engine rpm have built up to normal.

6. Be on the lookout for more icing and at frequent intervals apply carburetor heat to prevent a serious build-up of ice.

PART III. BACKGROUND INFORMATION

Engine Icing

Carburetor icing is known to be the cause of a great many flying accidents although the true number may never be ascertained because after an accident the evidence rapidly melts away.

The effects of carburetor icing on a piston engine are twofold—

    (a) a disturbance of the fuel/air ratio leading to a rich mixture condition which will ultimately stop the engine (rich mixture cut), and

    (b) a solid build-up of ice that will eventually prevent movement of the throttle.

Although it is the practice to talk in terms of carburetor icing there are in fact three separate types of ice formation which can adversely affect a piston engine using the conventional type of carburetor. These are—

        throttle icing
        impact icing
        fuel-evaporation icing

THROTTLE ICING

Anyone who has owned a bicycle must at some time have noticed
how the pump becomes warm while inflating a tire. This is common knowledge although the reason for the heat, apparently coming from nowhere, is not always understood. In practical as opposed to academic terms by compressing air the heat contained is
concentrated into a smaller volume. In effect the amount of heat
per unit volume has increased and heat per unit volume is another
way of saying temperature. Conversely when, by any means, the
pressure is reduced allowing a volume of air to expand the heat
within that volume becomes diluted and the temperature drops.
This is the meaning of **adiabatic heating** and **cooling** (Fig. 18).

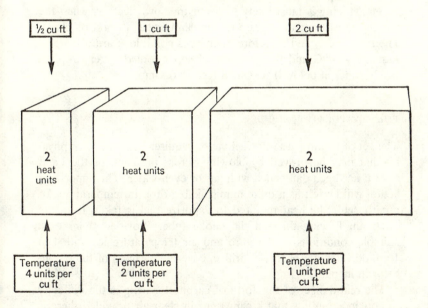

Fig. 18. Adiabatic heating and cooling showing the effect on
temperature of compressing and expanding one cubic foot of
air containing a fixed amount of heat.

It is part of the function of a carburetor to vaporize fuel so that
it will mix with air in the correct proportion for combustion. The
process occurs in the choke tube which utilizes the venturi princi-

ple to cause a decrease in pressure in the area of the fuel jet. This pressure drop and the associated decrease in temperature are at their greatest while the throttle is at small openings with the attendant risk of freezing whatever moisture is present in the air. Therefore throttle icing is most likely to occur at low power settings during say, stalling practice, a descent or while on a glide approach.

IMPACT ICING

This is caused when moist air comes into contact with parts of the induction system that are themselves below freezing temperature, e.g. the air intake and scoop, hot/cold air valve, carburetor screen, fuel jets and the throttle itself.

Impact icing is most likely to occur in snow, sleet or, when the correct moisture/temperature relationship exists, in rain or cloud. The most ideal, and therefore dangerous conditions are a temperature of $-4°$ C and the presence of super-cooled water droplets, liquid water at below $0°$ C which freezes on impact.

FUEL-EVAPORATION ICING

The act of turning gas into fuel vapor requires heat, a law of physics that may be proved by blowing across the back of the hand after it has been dampened with gas or even water. The vaporizing action will be felt as a quite unmistakable drop in temperature. In a carburetor the heat required to vaporize fuel is taken from the airstream flowing through the choke tube. Provided there exist suitable conditions of moisture and air temperature ice will then form downstream of the jet orifice, covering all parts of the carburetor in its path.

The real danger of this form of carburetor icing is the difficulty of convincing pilots that it can occur in clear air provided there is a minimum humidity of 60 per cent. Higher humidity increases the risk still further.

The combined effects of these three forms of carburetor icing may be summarized by saying that one way or another engine icing can occur within a temperature range of $+30°$ C and $-18°$ C, a high humidity providing moisture to be frozen in the choke tube will intensify the risk and the carburetor is most prone to icing while at small throttle settings.

DESIGN FEATURES FOR THE PURPOSE OF AVOIDING CARBURETOR ICING

The obvious way to prevent carburetor icing is to eliminate the carburetor and substitute another device for mixing fuel and air. There is, in fact, a growing use of fuel injection (into the cylinders) which not only eliminates throttle and fuel evaporation icing but also meters the fuel more accurately and economically than the conventional carburetor. However the possibility of impact icing remains and in larger aircraft this is sometimes dealt with by having an electrically heated air intake. More usually there is a wire mesh screen fitted ahead of the air intake and should the screen become covered in impact snow or ice air will continue to enter around the sides. In extreme cases of impact icing the gap between screen and air intake may become blocked when an alternate air source from within the engine cowling may be selected.

Most light aircraft of the single-engine type are still powered by a piston engine fitted with a carburetor and the prevention and removal of carburetor ice is catered for by providing a heated air supply through a large plate valve which is operated from the cabin by the carburetor heat control. In the "cold" (in) position cold air enters the carburetor through the filter in the normal way. When "hot" is selected the plate valve blanks off the cold air supply to the carburetor substituting air that has been passed through a heat exchanger, a simple box structure built around the exhaust manifold (Fig. 19). From the description it must be clear that a supply of hot air only exists so long as the engine itself is developing power. An engine that has failed completely as a result of carburetor icing will rapidly cool leaving no heat for the dispersal of ice formed in the choke tube.

USE OF CARBURETOR HEAT

A Shakespeare of the aviation world could be forgiven for writing "to use or not to use, that is the question" for so much has appeared in print on the subject of carburetor heat, much of it offering conflicting advice. This is hardly surprising because for some

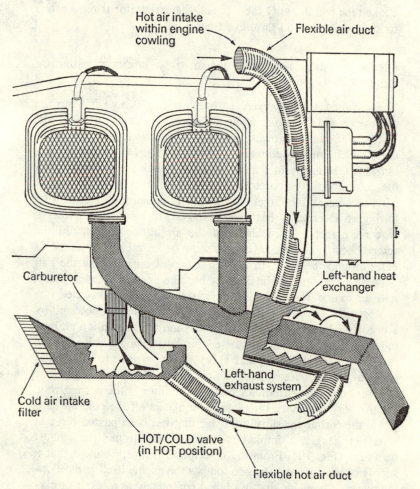

Hot air intake within engine cowling

Flexible air duct

Carburetor

Left-hand heat exchanger

Cold air intake filter

Left-hand exhaust system

HOT/COLD valve (in HOT position)

Flexible hot air duct

Fig. 19. Typical carburetor heat system. A similar heat exchanger is situated on the right-hand exhaust system.

years two systems were in use, each requiring different handling although the same instructions were often given for both.

Quite separate from the "hot air" provision that is a feature of most low-powered engines of American origin is the "warm air" system favored by European engine manufacturers. This dispenses with the need for a heat exchanger by simply drawing air from within the engine bay. Often the warm/cold valve was linked with the throttle so that cold air was available for take-off, while at cruising and lower power settings the engine inhaled warm air. Certainly the system worked well in so far as in northern Europe carburetor icing was virtually unknown in the aircraft so fitted, and indeed it would be reasonable to ask why the arrangement was discontinued in favor of the present manual selection of "hot" as opposed to "warm" air. There are several reasons for this, one of them being the need for fuel economy. A piston engine derives power by heating and expanding air within the confines of its cylinders, the greater the expansion the greater the power produced. One way of attaining a good expansion is to pack the cylinders with cold and therefore dense air. Any attempt to preheat the air must result in a reduction in the weight of charge induced into the cylinders and a consequent reduction in expansion which entails a corresponding loss of engine power. When "hot" air is introduced the decrease in power is of sufficient proportion to cause a reduction in engine speed of several hundred rpm. It is of course true that in cruising flight this loss of power may be restored by opening the throttle but this will entail a marked increase in fuel consumption. Thus when maximum power or economic cruising/climbing power is required air entering the cylinders must be as cold (and therefore dense) as possible.

While in North European climates the automatic use of warm air during cruising flight represented a satisfactory compromise between freedom from icing and fuel economy, there are many parts of the world where the prevailing temperature/humidity levels are such that the modest temperature rise of the "warm air" system had the effect of lifting the carburetor air temperature into the icing range and so causing the very hazard it was intended to prevent. This was one of the reasons for the introduction of "hot air." It would, however, be impracticable to link such a system to the throttle because—

(a) the loss of fuel economy while in cruising flight would be unacceptable, and

(b) in warm summer temperatures prolonged cruising in "hot air" can result in the engine overheating when detonation will occur.

It has therefore become almost universal practice to provide a separate control for carburetor heat. The question is how to use it. When a carburetor air-temperature gauge is fitted guesswork is eliminated, it being relatively easy to adjust the heat control until the temperature is safely out of the icing range. Various temperatures are obtainable by using the heat control in intermediate positions, when the plate valve will admit to the carburetor a mixture of hot and cold air as required. Without a carburetor air-temperature gauge the pilot is more or less in the dark about the state of his induction system until ice has formed sufficiently to affect the performance of the engine; therefore the only course available is to obey certain rules and adopt the routines set out below—

Phase of Flight	*Use of Carb. Heat*
STARTING AND TAXIING	Always use cold air. The air filter is bypassed when "hot" is selected and there is a risk of grit, etc., being ingested by the engine.
ENGINE RUN-UP	Always check the carb. heat (usually at 1,800–2,000 rpm). There should be a drop in rpm when full heat is applied or, in the case of a constant-speed propeller, a drop in manifold pressure. Should these indications be followed by an increase in reading *before* returning to cold air there has been ice and this must be regarded as evidence of severe carburetor icing at low levels.
TAKE-OFF	It is good practice to apply full heat for several seconds immediately before take-off. This is particularly important when there is high humidity.
	In extreme cases, e.g. the presence of freezing rain, use heat as instructed in the operating manual, provided the take-off performance is adequate for the available run allowing for

Phase of Flight	*Use of Carb. Heat*
	the power reduction that will result from applying carb. heat.
	Use of carb. heat for take-off is confined to abnormal conditions only. Normally the take-off must be performed in cold air.
CLIMB	Be prepared for carburetor icing when the humidity is known to exceed 60 per cent or while climbing through cloud, snow or freezing rain. When a carb. air-temperature gauge is fitted apply sufficient heat to keep out of the icing range. When there is no gauge apply full heat at intervals leaving it on for five seconds or so, a period long enough to show an increase in rpm when icing is present.
CRUISING	Adopt a similar procedure to the climb.
FLIGHT	Under all conditions it is important to make regular ice checks by applying full heat unless there is a carb. air-temperature gauge when the correct temperature may be set.
STALLING, SPINNING, GLIDING	Apply full heat before any maneuver entailing closing the throttle and leave it on until power is resumed. During prolonged glides, open the throttle at intervals to prevent over cooling. Remember there can be no carburetor heat from a cold engine.

Phase of Flight	*Use of Carb. Heat*
POWERED DESCENT	Treat like the climb.
ENGINE ASSISTED APPROACH AND LANDING	Always check for carb. ice by applying full heat on the downwind leg but return to "cold" for the approach. This is particularly important on a hot day when carb. heat is likely to cause detonation.
	When severe icing conditions are known to exist full heat should be used on the approach, or when a temperature gauge is fitted use sufficient heat to maintain a safe carb. air temperature.
GO-AROUND	Unless severe icing conditions are known to exist use cold air to obtain maximum power.
AFTER LANDING	During the postlanding checks ensure that the heat control is in the "cold" position (see "Starting and Taxiing" on page 122).

The foregoing instructions are not so complicated as they may at first appear. In essence they amount to this—

1. Unless severe icing conditions are known to exist use "cold" air whenever the engine is at a moderate to maximum power setting.

2. In *all* weather apply full heat before closing the throttle completely.

3. During the climb, cruise and powered descent make regular checks for ice.

4. Except for the purpose of testing the carb. heat during an engine run-up always use cold air while on the ground— remember that air filter (page 122).

5. Without the benefit of a carb. air-temperature gauge never use a "warm" setting (i.e. an intermediate position on the carb.

heat control) since this may have the effect of raising the temperature into the icing range rather than above it.

SYMPTOMS OF CARBURETOR ICING

While the warning signs associated with carburetor icing may differ in detail from one engine installation to another, in all cases the first stages take the form of a gradual power loss. When the aircraft has a constant-speed propeller the rpm will remain unchanged although there will be a reduction in manifold pressure due to the throttling action of the ice build-up. In the cruise there will be a tendency for all aircraft to lose height or, when this is arrested by retrimming nose-up, a loss of airspeed. If ice is allowed to accumulate, the ensuing rich mixture will cause rough running and, in the final stages, complete power loss due to the rich mixture cut already mentioned earlier in the text.

DISPERSING CARBURETOR ICING

Carburetor icing in the early stages of its formation will rapidly disperse when full heat is applied. On the other hand if the situation is allowed to reach the stage where rough running is unmistakable, accompanied by a severe power loss, the initial effect of applying carburetor heat may appear to worsen the matter. There is the further decline in power associated with hot air (page 120), the further richening of an already overrich mixture and the ingestion into the cylinders of melted ice and water. Small wonder that at first the cure seems worse than the illness. Even so the temptation to return the carburetor heat control to "cold" must be resisted because when the engine freezes to a halt there may be no green fields below as there were for Ron in Part I.

A large build-up of ice has the effect of altering the shape of the choke tube so that attempts to move the throttle, if indeed it can be moved at all, are likely to stall the airflow and possibly stop the engine when it may prove impossible to restart. In the advanced stages of carburetor icing an engine is rather like a dying fire and if prompt action is not taken it may become so cold that no heat exists to melt the ice. A contributing factor is that rich mixture has the effect of lowering an engine's working temperature. This being the case it must follow that a weak mixture will produce a reverse effect. Therefore in serious cases of carburetor icing the engine temperature should be increased by gradually leaning the mixture, taking care not to stop the engine by overleaning. Cooling air may be reduced by climbing at a low airspeed (weather permitting). If it is necessary to adjust the throttle, only to do so after the power has returned to near normal—and having cleared the engine of ice, take good care not to get caught again!

Airframe Icing

Most single-engine light aircraft, and for that matter many of the light twins, are not equipped to fly in conditions likely to cause airframe icing. Therefore when an aircraft of this kind is exposed to severe icing the situation that follows could well develop into an emergency in the true meaning of the word. There are four main types of airframe ice and they may occur while the aircraft is flying or even when it is on the ground. It is also quite possible to experience more than one kind of ice at the same time.

The main types of airframe icing are—

> **hoar frost**
> **rime ice**
> **clear ice**
> **freezing rain**

Hoar Frost. This is likely to occur on parts of the aircraft that have been cooled to a temperature below freezing. When air carrying excess water vapor comes into contact with these surfaces a light feather-like coating of ice will form. It may often be seen on aircraft that have been standing in the open during a clear, cold night. Having little thickness this type of ice is of low weight but the resultant skin friction may be of sufficient consequence to impair take-off performance. Hoar frost will obscure the windshield and windows and it may also affect the radio aerials; therefore before take-off it must be removed using an ice dispersing spray, or a hot air jet when one is available. This important precaution is not always treated seriously, although the consequences of an attempted take-off while carrying ice may be failure to lift off followed by extensive damage to the aircraft. Indeed the test for the instrument rating presupposes that the aircraft has been standing in the open overnight and failure to make the following checks for all types of ice constitutes an automatic fail—

1. Check all flying surfaces.

2. Check the controls are free to move, looking for ice in the control gaps (see Fig. 21, page 129).

3. Check static vents.

4. Check pressure or pitot head and vents.

5. Check that all drain holes are clear.

6. Check the aerials and insulators for ice.

7. Check windshield and windows.

In flight hoar frost will form on an aircraft that has been flying in a region below freezing temperature before entering a warmer and more humid air mass. As a result there is likely to be an increase in stalling speed, frost on the windshield and possibly some interference with the radio. As the airframe assumes the temperature of the surrounding warmer air the coating of hoar frost will rapidly disappear.

Rime Ice. To use its correct name, opaque rime ice is formed when supercooled water droplets come into contact with the airframe, usually while flying through a cloud containing this type of moisture. At ground level it is known as freezing fog. In appearance rime ice is a rough, white, opaque deposit growing forward into the oncoming airstream from the leading edges of the wings, tail surfaces, struts, aerials, etc. Since rime forms instantly on contact with the surface large amounts of air are trapped in countless minute pockets so that a quite substantial build-up of this type of ice weighs little. Its prime effect is to alter the aerodynamic shape and disturb the laminar flow around the wings and tail surfaces.

Clear Ice. This is sometimes known as translucent rime. The difference between this and the rime ice just described is that whereas opaque rime freezes instantly without spreading action, clear ice results from water supercooled to a temperature that allows it to flow during the freezing process and so build up a particularly dangerous and tenacious coating of clear, dense ice containing little trapped air (Fig. 20). This type of ice not only affects

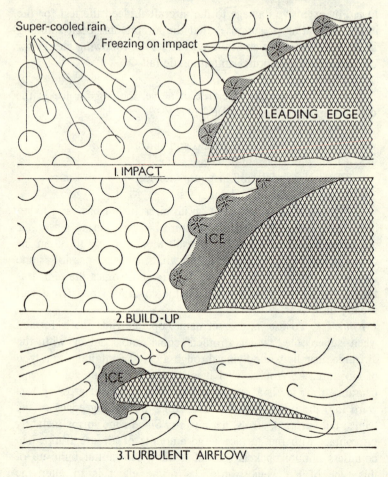

Fig. 20. Formation of clear ice.

the aerodynamics of the flying surfaces but also adds considerable weight to the airframe and propeller, in the latter case causing severe vibration.

Freezing Rain. Under certain conditions supercooled rain may occur beneath a warm front, occlusion or occasionally a cold front and an aircraft flying into this type of precipitation will collect clear ice. Usually the build-up will be very rapid and it must be regarded as a hazard to any light aircraft without airframe ice protection equipment.

THE EFFECTS OF AIRFRAME ICING

During the formation of all types of airframe icing the temperature of the aircraft surfaces is a more important factor than the temperature of the surrounding air. Ice is most likely to occur on thin rather than blunt, thick structures, hence the fact that the wings and tail surfaces are affected while in the main the fuselage remains free of ice.

The alteration in airfoil shape already described has the effect of increasing drag, decreasing lift and causing buffet, while a build-up on the fin and tailplane will seriously diminish the effectiveness of the controls. When the rudder, elevators and ailerons are of the shrouded type a severe build-up of ice may be sufficient to jam the controls (Fig. 21).

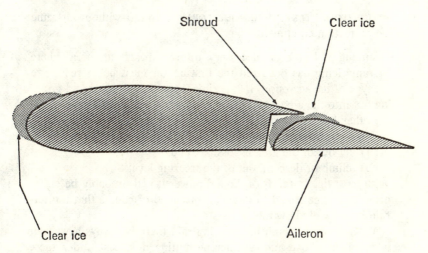

Fig. 21. Danger to controls affected by clear ice.

AVOIDING AIRFRAME ICING

When flying an aircraft not fitted with airframe ice protection equipment it makes sense to avoid the problem by flight planning in the first instance and by knowledge of the subject while in the air. A weather forecast will include the following information relevant to icing—

    (a) the freezing level (expressed in feet),

    (b) likelihood of icing expressed either as an icing index or in plain language thus—

          icing index light   or   light icing

          icing index moderate or   moderate icing

          icing index high   or   severe icing

Whenever it is expected that cloud will be entered in temperatures at or below 0° C pilots should expect airframe icing. The worst is likely to occur in cumulus type clouds although icing can be severe in nimbo-stratus. Airframe icing is least likely to occur when the air temperature is above 0° C or below —15° C. At low temperatures below freezing moisture will be in the form of ice crystals or snow, neither of which are likely to collect on the airframe.

ACTION TO BE TAKEN WHEN ICE FORMS (aircraft without airframe ice protection equipment)

Assuming it has been necessary to fly through an area where airframe icing has occurred the first action must be to recognize the type of ice accretion. If it is rime, i.e. white, opaque and growing out into the airstream, most likely icing will not be severe. On the other hand clear ice will develop very rapidly and immediate action must be taken to—

    (a) fly out of the area if possible, and

    (b) climb or descend out of the freezing level.

With most light aircraft of limited power it will probably be easier after ice has collected to descend, provided of course that the terrain below will allow this.

When a front is emitting freezing rain there is always a warmer layer of air above and weather permitting it is best under these conditions to climb above the cloud base. On no account fly parallel to a front of this kind in freezing rain. These are ideal conditions for the formation of clear ice!

When airframe icing conditions appear to extend over a considerable area of the country never fly on and hope the ice will go away. Call the FIR controller without delay and ask for his assistance. He will most likely provide headings to steer for an area where a descent below freezing level may be made in safety.

AIRFRAME ICING PROTECTION EQUIPMENT

Although there have been great improvements in the design of airframe icing protection equipment the basic concept and some of the methods used have remained unchanged for many years. The equipment falls under one of two headings.

Anti-icing, used to protect areas of the aircraft that may be critical to even slight ice accretion. In other words anti-icing equipment is intended to prevent the formation of ice.

De-icing is used to protect less vulnerable areas of the airframe from a heavy build-up of ice by breaking it away at intervals.

Anti-icing Equipment. The simplest anti-icing equipment, which in fact may be found on the majority of modern light aircraft, is the pitot heater, a component that must be kept free of ice at all times. Other areas that require similar protection are the windshield and, on high performance jet aircraft, the air intakes. While this form of anti-icing equipment is only to be found on larger and more complex aircraft the system is the same as that embodied in the pitot heater, i.e. an electric current is used to warm a heater element which raises the temperature of the surface to above $0°$ C, so preventing the adhesion of ice. Such a system makes heavy demands on the electric supply and circuit and is therefore not practical for a light aircraft.

De-icing Equipment. Typical areas protected by de-icing equipment are the leading edges of the wings, fin and tailplane, the methods used being—

    ice dispersing fluid (usually glycol or ethyl-alcohol)

    thermal (utilizing engine heat)

    spraymat (a form of electric heating)

    pneumatic

By adopting an intermittent cycle the fluid, heat, electric current, pneumatic pressure (according to the system in use) is conserved, thus allowing the aircraft to continue flying in icing conditions throughout its maximum endurance or range. The equipment is designed to allow a modest build-up of ice which is then removed at intervals before it can reach dangerous proportions.

Light aircraft de-icing equipment is almost invariably of the pneumatic type where rubber "boots" fitted to the wing and tail

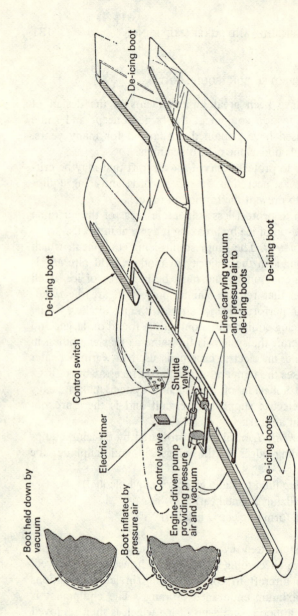

De-icing boot

De-icing boot

De-icing boot

De-icing boot

Control switch

Electric timer

Control valve

Engine-driven pump
providing pressure
air and vacuum

Shuttle
valve

Lines carrying vacuum
and pressure air to
de-icing boots

De-icing boots

Boot held down by
vacuum

Boot inflated by
pressure air

Fig. 22. De-icing installation.

Operation is as follows: In normal flight vacuum delivered from the engine pumps is conducted to the de-icing boots, thus holding them against the leading-edge contours. Operation of the control switch activates the timer which energizes the control valve, passing pressure air into the shuttle valve which then inflates the boots for several seconds. The timer again energizes the control valve which this time allows the shuttle valve to pump pressure air and once again apply vacuum to the boots. The cycle is repeated by the electric timer until the control switch is turned off.

surface leading edges are inflated and deflated by a cycling valve, breaking away the ice build-up at intervals that may be controlled by the pilot according to conditions. Pressure air for the system may be supplied from a ground-charged air bottle or, in some cases, engine-driven pumps (Fig. 22). The installation of de-icing boots entails a small penalty in the form of decreased payload and a slightly lower cruising speed.

PROPELLER DE-ICING EQUIPMENT

The propeller blades are, in effect, rotating wings and their leading edges are susceptible to ice accretion in much the same way as the wings and tail surfaces, in this case with the attendant risk of imbalance and therefore vibration. Propeller de-icing embodies a reservoir of ice dispersing fluid (glycol or ethyl-alcohol), a small electric pump controllable by the pilot and a slinger ring fitted with nozzles arranged to discharge the fluid onto rubber linings fixed to the leading edges of the propeller blades. When icing is detected (usually by the vibration) the de-icing equipment should be used before the ice build-up reaches such proportions that its removal causes large pieces to be flung against the fuselage—when damage to the airframe skin has been known to occur.

All airframe ice protection equipment must be checked during the preflight inspection. When the ice begins to form is not the time to discover that there is no pressure in the air bottle!

CONCLUSIONS

Provided the simple rules summarized on page 124 are observed no pilot should ever be caught off guard by carburetor icing. The situation with airframe icing is quite simply this. Learn to use the anti-icing and de-icing equipment available on the aircraft and to appreciate the conditions likely to induce airframe icing. When there is no ice protection equipment and icing conditions are expected, keep the aircraft on the ground.

CHAPTER 11

Loss of Primary Instruments

PART I. THE SITUATION

It was one of those flying clubs where the only religion practiced was in the name of aerobatics. The boys and girls talked, ate and worshipped rolls, loops and combination maneuvers to the exclusion of all other aspects of flying, or for that matter anything else. Radio was an intrusion, twin flying another world while instrument flying was regarded as a bore—a bad joke concocted by those who had to fly from A to B to pay the rent. In fairness the club had produced quite a number of good aerobatic pilots and up among the talented was a young lad named Charles. One has to admire the aerobatic breed for their dedication and the amount of practice they put in, but it was in the course of perfecting a new sequence that Charles almost bit the dust—although it was his disdain for instrument flying rather than a passion for aerobatics that all but cost him his life.

The day it happened many of the usual crowd were at the airfield and most of them saw Charles take off. Forty minutes later he appeared low in the pattern, landed, then walked to the club looking white and shaken where he booked in before driving home without so much as a "good-bye" to his club mates. At first only a few of his closest friends were in the know but later the story became common knowledge. It went something like this.

When Charles took off for his practice aerobatics there was a broken layer of cloud covering the area at about 1,500 ft. The airfield was situated well away from controlled airspace so young Charles very wisely decided to climb through the blue bits and practice his sequence over the top. After twenty minutes or so he became aware that the broken cloud had become a solid white carpet. Fortunately this particular aircraft had VOR and he was able to position himself over a conveniently situated beacon but he was, all or nothing, an aerobatic man and the thought of having to let down on instruments through 2,000 ft. of cloud was one that hardly filled him with enthusiasm.

For the first time he noticed that his Artificial Horizon was thrashing around random fashion. "Bloody fool manufacturers. Fancy putting an instrument that will tumble in an aerobatic airplane," he told himself with some justification. Of course he had seen this happen before and thought little of it. In any case after a time the horizon had always erected again, so he flew around and waited—and waited, and waited and waited, while the horizon bar continued to dance about with undiminished frenzy. No instrument pilot, at least Charles was a realist and he began to prepare himself for a descent through cloud on the partial panel, something he had read about but never done! Fortunately he knew his position and there was no high ground for many miles. And he comforted himself with the thought that there was enough fuel to reach an airfield with radar—not that he had ever tried that either. But first he would attempt to get through near the beacon.

He let down to cloud top level, trimmed out at eighty then reduced power for the descent, forgetting that closing the throttle would upset the trim. Almost immediately he was in the blinding whiteness and he sat there, gripping the stick far too tightly, eyes glued to the turn-and-slip indicator while the fear of the unknown began to play its evil game. "Speed too high—back with the stick —watch that rate two turn to the left—right rudder—no right aileron—that's better—*look at that airspeed*—mustn't stall—forward on the stick, *forward*." Despite a seat belt that had been tightened for aerobatics he left the seat while lunging forward on the stick. By now sickness threatened, his hands were hot and damp and a wringing wet shirt adhered to his back. For a moment he gathered his wits and tried to take in the instrument panel, at first forgetting that the artificial horizon was out of business and to be ignored. The ball was over to the left and he kicked on full right rudder. Things were going very wrong for Charles. The airspeed was coming up to "never exceed" and the engine had waved farewell to the red line.

At a thousand feet he came out of cloud in a screaming spiral dive. By the time he had sorted things out most of that had gone and Charles had to climb again to become legal. He felt cold and his hands and legs were shaking. At first he could make nothing of the VOR, then he reset his DG and crept home a wiser man convinced that even aerobatic pilots should be able to fly on the partial panel. Come to think of it their need is as great as any other pilot's because gyros do tumble during aerobatics. Or perhaps it would be more correct to say that the ability to fly on the partial panel should be part of every pilot's skill. A tumbled artificial horizon or a faulty directional gyro is something that can happen to anyone.

PART II. THE PROCEDURE

(NOTE. Throughout the following text the turn-and-slip indicator is referred to as a needle-and-ball. Other presentations, such as the two-needle display or the Turn Co-ordinator may be used in the same manner.)

There has been a failure of the vacuum-driven directional gyro and the artificial horizon and it is necessary to fly through cloud using a partial panel comprising an electric turn-and-slip indicator, the ASI, the altimeter, the VSI and the magnetic compass.

Straight and Level Flight

MAINTAINING HEIGHT AND AIRSPEED

1. At the correct power setting and airspeed carefully trim the aircraft.

2. Hold the stick gently and allow the aircraft to fly itself using small pressures on the elevator control to adjust the airspeed.

3. Small deviations from cruising level may be corrected with the elevator but larger height adjustments will require the use of throttle.

4. When the airspeed is correct but height is being lost, increase power slightly and, if necessary, retrim. Conversely when height is being gained at the correct airspeed reduce power slightly and re-trim.

5. Avoid overcorrecting, which can only lead to "chasing the airspeed and altimeter."

MAINTAINING DIRECTION

1. Using the turn-and-slip indicator concentrate on keeping the wings level by controlling the turn needle with aileron. Maintain balance by using rudder in the direction indicated by the ball which must be kept in the center.

2. To hold a required heading, refer to the magnetic compass but make allowance for compass error.

3. Allow the ailerons to ride free using gentle pressures to correct turn needle indications, e.g. left needle requires right aileron.

4. At intervals check the compass heading ensuring that the wings are level and the airspeed is steady before taking a reading.

5. Avoid overcorrecting which can only lead to "chasing the compass."

CLIMBING

1. With the turn-and-slip indicator showing no turn and in balance, open the throttle to climbing power.

2. Check the ball for indications of skid and correct with rudder.

3. Gently and progressively raise the nose while watching the airspeed indicator, retrim at the correct speed.

4. Check the turn needle and keep the wings level with aileron. Check the ball and if necessary correct with rudder.

5. Only when the airspeed has settled, check the heading on the compass and if necessary correct by using aileron in the appropriate direction.

RETURNING TO STRAIGHT AND LEVEL FLIGHT

1. Gently and progressively ease forward the stick while watching the airspeed indicator.

2. With reference to the turn needle check that the wings are level. Keep the ball in the center with rudder.

3. As cruising speed is approached, throttle back to the correct power setting, then retrim. Make small attitude adjustments to hold the correct airspeed and if necessary adjust the throttle.

4. Check the trim again.

5. Check the heading on the magnetic compass and make whatever adjustments are necessary.

DESCENDING

1. With the turn-and-slip indicator showing no turn and in balance, reduce power to an rpm setting known to produce the required rate of descent.

2. Check the ball for indications of skid and if necessary correct with rudder.

3. Gently, and progressively, hold back the stick while watching the airspeed indicator. Retrim at the correct powered descent speed.

4. Check the turn needle and keep the wings level with aileron.

5. Only when the airspeed has settled check the heading on the magnetic compass and if necessary, correct by using aileron in the appropriate direction.

RETURNING TO STRAIGHT AND LEVEL FLIGHT

1. Shortly before the required cruising level open the throttle to the correct rpm.

2. Make the usual checks for level and balance using the turn-and-slip indicator in conjunction with aileron and rudder.

3. Gently and progressively ease forward on the stick while watching the airspeed indicator.

4. At cruising speed retrim, then check rpm, height and heading making such adjustments as are necessary.

TURNS ON THE LIMITED PANEL

1. Determine the number of degrees to the new heading and convert these to seconds, allowing 3° per second (Rate 1 turn).

2. Gently move the ailerons in the direction of the turn and start the watch (or begin counting at second intervals).

3. As the turn needle indicates Rate 1 move the ailerons to the neutral position. Check balance with reference to the ball and if necessary correct with rudder.

4. Guard against loss of height by applying gentle back pressure to the elevators.

5. When the required number of seconds has elapsed gently roll out of the turn by applying aileron in the opposite direction. Allow the stick to resume its trimmed position.

6. Check the heading on the magnetic compass and make such minor adjustments as may be necessary.

Recovery from Unusual Attitudes

THE DIVE

While flying in cloud on the limited panel the aircraft enters turbulence, the airspeed begins to increase rapidly and there is a high rate of descent. The aircraft is in a dive—and the following actions are needed.

1. Check the turn-and-slip indicator and if necessary level the wings with aileron.

2. Progressively and gently move the stick back until the airspeed stops increasing. Continue the back pressure until the ASI needle moves towards cruising speed, then firmly hold the attitude on the elevators. The aircraft is now near the level attitude.

3. Allow the speed to settle, then check rpm, trim and heading.

HIGH NOSE-UP ATTITUDE

It is noticed that the airspeed is decreasing rapidly and there is a high rate of climb. The aircraft is in a steep nose-up attitude—the following actions are needed.

1. Check the turn-and-slip indicator and if necessary level the wings with aileron.

2. Progressively and gently move the stick forward until the airspeed stops decreasing. Continue the forward pressure until the ASI needle moves towards cruising speed, then firmly hold this attitude with the elevators. The aircraft is now near the level attitude.

3. Allow the speed to settle, then check the rpm, trim and heading.

RECOVERY FROM THE SPIN

1. Close the throttle, then check the direction of yaw on the turn needle and determine that it is a spin and not a spiral dive.

2. Apply full rudder opposite to the yaw indicated on the turn needle.

3. After a brief pause, ease forward the stick until the turn needle deflects fully to the opposite side of the instrument before centralizing, thus indicating that spinning has stopped. The airspeed will now rapidly increase.

4. Centralize the rudder, then level the wings using aileron in conjunction with the turn needle and center the ball with rudder.

5. Gently ease the airplane out of the dive using the method already described (the Dive, page 139).

RECOVERY FROM A SPIRAL DIVE

1. Close the throttle, then check the direction of spiral on the turn needle and determine that it is a spiral dive and not a spin.

2. Level the wings using the ailerons in conjunction with the turn needle and center the ball with rudder.

3. Ease the aircraft out of the dive using the method already described (the Dive, page 139).

PART III. BACKGROUND INFORMATION

Had this book been written during the 1920s flying on the partial panel would have been regarded as normal. In those days even quite large aircraft had no more than an ASI, a form of spirit level and a simple altimeter with a single finger reading at intervals of 200 ft. Within a few years the Reid and Sigrist turn-and-bank indicator (as it was then called) was introduced, an instrument that compares very favorably with its modern equivalent. Certainly as late as 1945 thousands of RAF pilots were being taught the instrument take-off with complete success on these beautifully damped instruments, without the assistance of an artificial horizon or directional gyro. However, yesterday's luxuries are tomorrow's minimum requirements and today the light airplane without a full flight panel is the exception, rather than the rule. Under the circumstances it would be reasonable to ask why any pilot should devote time and effort to doing things the hard way, for without doubt the partial panel is a harder taskmaster than the full flight panel. The short answer is that the turn-and-slip indicator will continue to give valuable information after the other gyro instruments have exceeded their limits or failed.

Possible Causes of Gyro Instrument Failure

Gyro instruments may be either vacuum or electrically driven and the most likely causes of malfunction are—

Vacuum Type	*Electric Type*
Failure of vacuum supply	Failure of electric supply
Blocked filter	Blown fuse of tripped circuit breaker
Exceeding tumbling limits	Exceeding tumbling limits
Mechanical fault	Mechanical fault

VACUUM SUPPLY

Most aircraft with a full flight panel are fitted with an engine-driven vacuum pump which supplies the instruments through an adjustable pressure-reduction valve. Sometimes there is a small drain cock (similar in appearance to a fuel strainer) for the purpose of clearing the vacuum system of unwanted oil or moisture and this should be operated before the first flight of the day. Failure of the vacuum pump, which will be confirmed by the vacuum gauge, is very rare indeed. In the case of a twin-engine aircraft there will be two pumps; therefore vacuum supply will continue with either inoperative. With most single-engine aircraft, however, loss of the only vacuum pump will mean loss of the vacuum-operated gyro instruments although some aircraft have an alternative vacuum source which is usually a venturi tube. The practice of using one of these tubes as the sole means of vacuum supply is now rare, the disadvantages being risk of ice forming on the venturi tube with the attendant loss of instruments and the absence of supply until the aircraft has been flying, thus preventing an instrument take-off.

BLOCKED FILTERS

Vacuum supply is led to the gyro instrument cases. Replacement air enters each instrument via a filter and then passes through jets which direct the air into "buckets" machined into the periphery of the gyro, which is rather like a small, high-speed water wheel using air for the driving force. Over a period of time these filters become clogged with foreign matter and eventually the flow of incoming air may be so restricted that the gyro will fail to reach the minimum rotational speed for accurate operation. Rotor speeds vary between 10,000 and 25,000 rpm according to the type of instrument. It is therefore important that these filters are serviced at regular intervals.

ELECTRIC INSTRUMENTS

One of the advantages of electric instruments is that the unit can be sealed and therefore protected from foreign matter which, over a period of time, will penetrate even a well-filtered vacuum-driven gyro and eventually cause damage to the high-precision bearings. Furthermore electric instruments perform well at high altitudes where vacuum systems are at a disadvantage because of the low air density. However an electric flight panel is dependent for its supply upon the aircraft's electric system and should there be a general power failure the consequence must be total loss of the flight panel. On large aircraft there is usually a standby artificial horizon with its own independent electric source, or there may be a set of vacuum-driven instruments. Loss of electrics as it applies to light single- and twin-engine aircraft is described in Chapter 8, page 90. Electric instruments sometimes incorporate an OFF warning flag and when only one instrument has failed there may be a blown fuse or a tripped circuit breaker due to a temporary electric overload. When attempts to reset the circuit breaker (or replace the fuse) result in another failure there is probably an instrument or wiring fault that requires attention on the ground.

MECHANICAL FAULTS

Generally the construction of gyro instruments is of a very high standard and actual mechanical failure as opposed to gradual deterioration through wear is unlikely—but not unknown. Such failures that do occur will almost without exception be unmistakable, an example being the artificial horizon mentioned in Part I.

EXCEEDING TUMBLING LIMITS

Because the gyros rotate in bearings and must also be free to alter their plane of rigidity in relation to the aircraft one or in some cases two **gimbal rings** are incorporated in the instrument according to its purpose. There is the added complexity of having to direct the air jet to the edge of the rotor so that movement of the rotor plane is in most instruments restricted, after which limit the gimbal affected will come up against a stop, the gyro will be upset and cease to operate in a rigid manner. The instrument is then said to have **tumbled.** Tumbling limits vary according to the type of instrument. For example the early Mk 1B artificial horizon allowed bank indications of up to 110° left or right and 60° pitch up or down. Later instruments improved on these limits and now certain artificial horizons allow complete freedom of indication in both as do some directional gyros. However when the instruments are not of this type both the artificial horizon and the directional gyro will tumble when the aircraft reaches an extreme attitude and while the DG may be erected immediately by the setting knob, most artificial horizons require up to ten minutes while automatic re-erection occurs. Should the **pendulous unit** responsible for this function be faulty, the instrument will cease to provide usable indications. Herein lies the value of the turn-and-slip indicator, an instrument devised many years ago that nevertheless continues to find a place on the flight panel of even the largest and most modern jet aircraft.

THE TURN-AND-SLIP INDICATOR

Unlike the artificial horizon or the directional gyro the turn-and-slip indicator gyro is required to move in one plane only. It may therefore be mounted in a single gimbal. Although there are limit stops the gyro will not tumble and since the gimbal is controlled by centering springs the instrument will continue to give accurate information as soon as the aircraft allows it to operate within limits. These are usually a Rate 4 turn left or right.

The balance or slip/skid part of the instrument is usually a simple pendulum or a ball and it is therefore independent of any outside supply source.

To further enhance the value of the turn-and-slip indicator as a standby instrument it has now become common practice to use electric drive so that it is independent of possible vacuum failure. It therefore follows that since the turn-and-slip indicator will continue to give valuable information after the other gyros have tumbled or perhaps failed as a result of lost vacuum, pilots would be well advised to learn how to fly on it during an emergency when there is no artificial horizon or directional gyro. Regrettably few pilots recognize the importance of this.

FLIGHT ON THE PARTIAL PANEL

Throughout Part II of this chapter the words "gentle," "gradual" and "progressive" frequently appear. Never are they more appropriate than when flying on the partial panel. Provided they are correctly trimmed most aircraft will fly themselves accurately "hands off" but many pilots have a tendency to grip the controls so hard that feel is lost. Light aircraft can only be flown accurately when the ailerons and elevators are controlled with the fingers, not the fist. All changes of attitude in the pitching and rolling plane or alterations of power should be introduced gradually, if necessary in stages, retrimming at each stage.

The partial panel is usually regarded as comprising the following instruments—

airspeed indicator
altimeter
magnetic compass
turn-and-slip indicator

In the event of a failure of the vacuum supply these instruments would in most aircraft be supplemented by the vertical speed indicator which, like the ASI and altimeter, is a pressure instrument.

USING THE VERTICAL SPEED INDICATOR

Correctly used the VSI will provide pitch information in so far as a slight attitude deviation from that required to maintain height will produce an immediate indication of climb or descent although several seconds will be required for the instrument to settle into an accurate reading. Violent changes in pitch can under certain circumstances produce a reverse reading and the importance of gradual attitude changes is once again stressed.

THE AIRSPEED INDICATOR

Contrary to the often misquoted belief, for all practical purposes there is no lag in the ASI. However like any other vehicle the airplane requires time to accelerate and decelerate.

When flying on the partial panel the airspeed indicator becomes the prime reference for pitch attitude. This will be understood if one of the basic principles of flight is recalled, i.e. at any given weight a particular airspeed will correspond to a particular angle of attack.

Because of inertia, time must be allowed for the aircraft to change from one airspeed to another.

THE ALTIMETER

Except during low rates of climb and descent this instrument suffers from lag, therefore during instrument flying on the full or partial panel descent rates should not normally exceed 500 ft. per minute. The function of the altimeter remains the same during normal visual flight or instrument flight. Intelligent use of the VSI will assist in holding a steady cruising altitude.

THE MAGNETIC COMPASS

Much has been written about the various errors that make the magnetic compass so difficult to use in an airplane. Since it is assumed that readers of this book are licensed pilots there is no need to explain these errors in detail but it would perhaps be of benefit to summarize the use of the magnetic compass in the air.

While Flying on Northerly and Southerly Headings. There is a northerly turning error which is at a maximum on North and South. Any maneuver that has the effect of tilting the magnet systems (e.g. a turn or a sideslip) will cause the "North" position on the compass card to move towards the lower wing. Therefore when checking a northerly or southerly heading it is important to ensure that the wings are level. The error applies in the reverse direction in the Southern Hemisphere.

When Flying on Easterly or Westerly Headings. There is an acceleration/deceleration error which is at a maximum on East and West. An acceleration will cause the "North" position on the compass card to swing towards the nose of the aircraft and a deceleration will cause a swing towards the tail. Therefore before checking an easterly or westerly heading on the magnetic compass, ensure that the airspeed is steady. The error applies in the reverse direction in the Southern Hemisphere.

USING THE TURN-AND-SLIP INDICATOR

As the sole gyro instrument on the partial panel the turn-and-slip indicator assumes particular importance. Correctly used it will provide the following information—

lateral level
balance and yaw
rate of turn

Because of the close relationship between yaw and roll to some extent there is an overlap of information provided by the turn needle and the ball and it is best to interpret the instrument as shown in Fig. 23.

Flying technique is based upon the principle that direction is controlled by the ailerons, therefore the turn needle is likewise controlled by the ailerons. Even on the full panel, pilots learning instrument flying usually have difficulty maintaining direction because insufficient attention is paid to holding the wings level; even one or two degrees of bank will start a gentle turn. If lateral level is vital for the maintenance of direction it is none the less so when limited to the turn-and-slip indicator. Since in turbulent conditions the magnetic compass may be confined to giving accurate readings during brief periods of level flight at a steady airspeed the turn needle should be used to maintain a required heading by adopting the following technique.

1. With the aircraft correctly trimmed and the ball in balance watch the turn needle.

2. If the needle deflects, say, to the left, move the ailerons to produce a similar deflection to the right.

3. Hold right bank for the same duration as the previous "left turn" indication before returning the needle to the center.

INTERPRETATION DURING SPINS AND SPIRAL DIVES

Given a reasonable degree of pilot skill it would require very severe turbulence or deliberate mishandling to cause an inadvertent spin or spiral dive. Should it happen the differences in instrument indications are—

	Spin	*Spiral Dive*
AIRSPEED	Low and perhaps fluctuating	Accelerating rapidly
TURN-AND-SLIP	High turn rate with the ball showing a skid	High turn rate with the ball in balance

In each case the altimeter and the VSI will show a high rate of descent.

Pressure Instrument Failure

The foregoing text has been confined to malfunction of the gyro instruments but, unless the aircraft has a heated pitot head, icing may cause loss of the following pressure-operated instruments—

ASI

altimeter

VSI

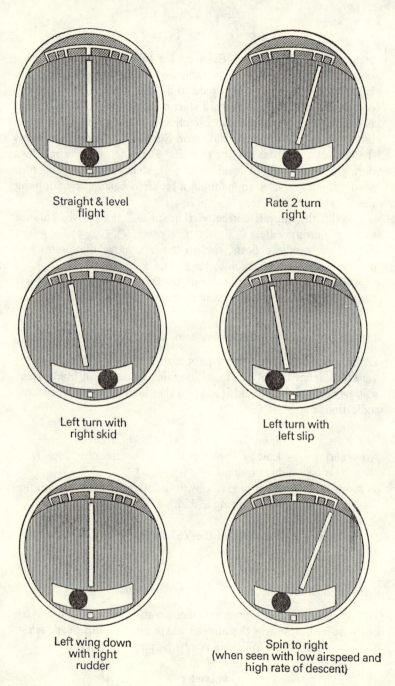

Straight & level
flight

Rate 2 turn
right

Left turn with
right skid

Left turn with
left slip

Left wing down
with right
rudder

Spin to right
(when seen with low airspeed and
high rate of descent)

Fig. 23. The turn-and-slip indicator.

Some modern light aircraft use a separate pressure head in conjunction with a fuselage-mounted **static vent** when icing, if it forms, will only affect pressure air. While in these cases the airspeed indicator will fail the altimeter and VSI should continue to function.

In a situation where both pressure and static supply is lost through icing of the pitot head, the altimeter may be rendered usable by breaking the glass of the VSI—which will then continue to give readings but in the reverse sense.

Action to Be Taken When the ASI Has Failed

1. Use the altimeter in the usual way to determine terrain clearance and, eventually, proximity to the landing area.

2. Use the artificial horizon to maintain attitude at a power setting known to produce the required airspeed.

3. Assuming the glass of the VSI has been broken (to restore use of the altimeter) read "up" for down and "down" for up.

CONCLUSIONS

The pessimist is entitled to ask, "What should I do if my gyros tumble and the ASI ceases to function?" To this question it would be equally fair to answer, "Without hope there can be no life." Instrument failure of any kind is rare and usually confined to either electric or vacuum loss (gyro instruments) or icing (pressure instruments). A combination of both would obviously demand landing as quickly as possible and when there are no holes in the clouds for the let-down the problem is indeed severe. Even so, with practice, the aircraft may be controlled on the turn-and-slip indicator, altimeter and magnetic compass provided the aircraft is correctly trimmed and the rpm are adjusted to known settings (i.e. for climb, straight and level, descent, etc.). Flying the airplane on these few instruments is a worthy practice—after which the partial panel will seem a not-so-difficult task after all! Charles would agree. He now flies well on the partial panel—and enjoys his aerobatics more than ever.

CHAPTER 12

Ditching

PART I. THE SITUATION

True Story No. 1

The company Apache, a nice gentlemanly little twin with quite adequate radio, took off one winter morning, joined the airways and headed for the Netherlands. The pilot, a young man of modest experience, had with him one passenger, bound for Rotterdam. The route forecast was neither good nor particularly bad; in fact the destination was going in for ⅔ cumulus, base 2,000 ft., 10 km visibility and winds of 290°/13 kt. becoming 320°/20–30 kt. With such a forecast the pilot could expect little difficulty at the terminal end and every likelihood of a visual let-down, approach and landing. However on this occasion the "actual," while following closely to the expected cumulus and visibility, included ⅞ stratocumulus which covered the area from a height of 3,500 ft. and in the events that followed, proved to be something of a nuisance.

Fifty-one minutes after take-off they were over the Clacton VOR and London handed them to Amsterdam ATC. So far the trip was running like clockwork. Then twenty-seven minutes later the pilot noticed that his radio was becoming weak and Amsterdam appeared not to be receiving his transmissions. Within min-

utes the VOR and the ADF had given up and in an effort to hold
the discharge shown on the ammeter and save the radio he began
switching off such home comforts as the cabin heater, the rotating
beacon and the rather essential pitot heater.

The forecast had said there would be large gaps in the clouds
over Holland but the uninvited stratocumulus thought differently
and the pilot therefore decided not to risk letting down into the
unknown over the Dutch countryside. The forecast was wrong so
how could he now be sure about the cloud base?

The company pilot turned back towards the Southend area
flying VFR on top and hoped that the weather would permit a let-
down in safety. Fortunately the flight panel was vacuum-operated
and therefore unaffected by the electric power fault. ETA Southend came and as he was still flying over ⅝ stratocumulus he tried
to attract radar attention by flying right-hand triangles with one-
minute legs, a NATO procedure supposed to produce another
"guide dog" aircraft. When after forty-five minutes nothing had
happened he decided to head east and plan a let-down over the
sea. By now his electric fuel gauges were reading empty although
there must have been enough in the tanks for another ninety minutes flying. The amber landing gear light had faded to a mere glow
and the end of the battery was near.

A welcome gap in the cloud appeared and he went through it to
find a cloud base of 500 ft. with mist running down to the sea
below. It seemed unsafe to attempt a landfall. A trawler appeared
out of the gloom and he flew past it lowering and raising his landing gear while at the same time altering his engine rpm to attract
attention. They had put on their life jackets and the pilot had told
his passenger what to expect in the ditching to come.

Down on the water the trawler skipper was quick to get the
message and immediately set about pulling in his nets. Up in the
aircraft they had wedged the cabin door open to avoid the risk of
jamming after ditching. A powered approach was begun at 65–70
kt., wheels and flaps up, the sea lying calm under a 5 kt. wind.

It was a gentle landing, the Apache decelerating quite smoothly
until at a low speed the nose went into the water and they came to
a sudden and decisive stop. The pilot and his passenger got out
and stood on the wing inflating their life jackets while the aircraft
rocked gently on the water where it floated in a more or less level

attitude. After two minutes it went down nose first and in no time at all the trawler had fished both pilot and passenger out of the water.

Since the fault was an electrical one and the vital evidence was likely to be obliterated by salt water no attempt was made to raise and inspect the aircraft, so to this day the cause of the power failure is not known. Sad to relate the pilot had unknowingly flown away from an area over the Netherlands where a let-down could have been made followed by a landing in VFR. But the official accident report says of the ditching—"This operation was carried out neatly and successfully." As indeed it was.

True Story No. 2

The club had decided to descend in force upon the unsuspecting French. It was quite a turn-out: a Cherokee 160 and a Super Rallye, both of them well equipped with radio, accompanied by three elderly Austers and a Turbulent. All the Austers had full flight panels and one of them had a 12-channel VHF set. The Turbulent was a simple affair limited to basic instruments and like the other two Austers, it had no radio.

The outward flight to Rouen was uneventful but on checking the weather the following day there was talk of fog patches in the Le Touquet area although they were expected to clear quite rapidly. To ensure that the less experienced pilots kept out of trouble on the return journey it was decided that the Cherokee and the Super Rallye would go on ahead and transmit back the weather to the radio-equipped Auster. This was being flown by an instructor and he would lead the other two Austers and the Turbulent in loose formation. Although the airfield at Le Treport was clearly seen the two leading aircraft encountered unexpected fog in the vicinity and a message to this effect was transmitted to the leader of the other four aircraft following some ten miles behind. The message was not acknowledged. Soon afterwards the Cherokee, by now somewhat ahead of the Rallye, ran into further dense patches of fog and these extended from sea level, blotting out Berck airfield where they had all arranged to meet. Again the flight conditions were radioed, this time advising a diversion to Le Treport which was known to be VFR. The Rallye acknowledged this message but again there was no word from the Auster.

At Le Treport the Cherokee taxied in to join the Rallye which had already landed and the two crews were just in time to see three Austers and a Turbulent bunched together and flying past at cliff top level, obviously heading for Berck and of course the fog. The Cherokee pilot switched on his radio and told the lead Auster to land at Le Treport. For almost forty minutes he repeated the message but to no avail; in fact it later transpired that the Auster had not been listening out as arranged. He continued transmitting until two of the Austers landed and broke the news. The leading aircraft and the Turbulent had been involved in an accident and it looked bad.

Low over the sea just off the French coast the leading Auster groped its way through the ever-changing fog which at times seemed to be dissolving, only to thicken again and blot out the world below. Alongside and desperately trying to keep the Auster in view was the Turbulent. Sitting with the pilot of the Auster was a professional simulator instructor while behind them was the pilot's wife. The man flying the aircraft, a wartime pilot in his mid-forties, had quite recently obtained his civil flying instructor's rating and although he had done quite a lot of flying those who knew him said he was a "seat-of-the-pants" aviator with a mistrust of instruments. He was to pay dearly for this.

While attempting a 180° turn towards a clearer patch the Auster stalled into the sea hitting the water within 400 ft. of the beach. At that point the Turbulent pilot gave up, attempted a landing on the soft sand, seriously damaging the aircraft and collecting a broken nose. Meanwhile the pilot had managed to get out of the sinking Auster and so had the simulator instructor who swam for the shore, there to be dragged from the water semi-conscious and given artificial respiration by two French fishermen. Passengers who flew in the rear of those early Austers gained access and exit by folding the front seat and crawling over. This involved lifting the seat back out of two retaining slots, a stiff and awkward task under normal circumstances and a near impossible one for an inexperienced passenger in a sinking aircraft. The pilot made desperate efforts to free his wife, without success, and her body was recovered off the Hook of Holland six months later.

He was never seen again. It happened so near the beach and all three were strong swimmers, yet only the simulator instructor survived.

PART II. THE PROCEDURE

While flying over the sea it becomes necessary to ditch the aircraft. It is assumed in this case that the engine is still functioning. Take steps as follows.

1. Warn the passengers that a ditching is necessary and enlist their help in securing or jettisoning any heavy objects on board.

2. Send out a "Mayday" call giving your position and intentions.

3. If possible aim to ditch near a ship, arranging to touch down ahead and to one side of the vessel.

4. Determine the surface wind and assess the direction of the swell. If the wind strength is less than 25 kt. land parallel with the swell. Head partly into wind and partly across the swell in wind speeds of between 25 and 35 kt. but land into wind when the wind speed exceeds 35 kt.

5. Approach with power at the lowest speed consistent with safety. Use the flaps as recommended for the aircraft type.

6. Unlatch the cabin doors and use a briefcase or similar object to keep them open.

7. In high-wing monoplanes open the cabin windows.

8. Have a cushion or folded coat ready to protect the face on touchdown.

9. Check that all seat belts are tight and that when available the shoulder straps are in use.

10. Remove all headsets and place them where the leads cannot obstruct exit from the aircraft.

11. Near the water aim to land in a tail-down attitude and use the throttle to place the aircraft on the crest of a large wave or swell or on a downslope. On no account fly into the face of a swell.

12. Shortly before touchdown protect the face using the means already prepared.

13. After touchdown hold back the stick, allow the aircraft to come to a halt, then open the doors and leave the cabin without delay.

14. After leaving the cabin, inflate the life jackets and the life raft (if carried), keep together and swim away from the aircraft—which is likely to sink within a few minutes.

15. Get into the life raft and make for the ship, using whatever signaling equipment is available to attract attention.

PART III. BACKGROUND INFORMATION

A light aircraft ditching is an experience not to be envied. It is an emergency affected by so many variables that the likelihood of success is difficult to forecast, a difficulty not alleviated by the obvious fact that ditching is not an exercise that can be practiced like a normal forced landing. It does, however, have this in common with most other emergencies: The best protection is avoidance by taking the correct precautions.

Preparing for Cross-water Flight

Preflight checks are always important. They are never more so than when a water crossing is involved and particular attention must be paid to the provision of adequate fuel for the journey. When flying a single-engine aircraft always plan to cross the shortest possible distance over water. The flying fraternity is full of valiant pilots who make a regular habit of ignoring this golden rule, yet the saving of a little flying time must surely be poor compensation for the risk involved in relying on a single engine over the open sea.

It is not only essential to carry life jackets; they should be worn, at least until the water crossing has been completed. Furthermore there is little point in wearing life jackets unless all occupants of the aircraft are fully aware of the inflating procedure. A ditching is not the time to find out; someone may fail to inflate his jacket in the water, or, possibly even worse, he could inflate it in the aircraft and then find it impossible to get through the cabin door.

Experience has shown that even the strongest swimmer cannot survive in a near freezing sea, because after five or ten minutes he will be too stiff to swim. It is therefore prudent to carry an inflatable life raft when there is a cold sea to be crossed. Life rafts may usually be hired for the purpose. They should be stowed where they can be reached in an emergency and not where the sea can drive them down the fuselage in the event of the windshield bursting on impact, a complication that is by no means unknown.

A great variety of safety equipment can be purchased from the specialist flying equipment shops, some of it quite inexpensive. Here are some of the items that should be considered when a long water crossing is planned—

> fluorocrine dye (to mark the sea and aid location and rescue)
> flares
> smoke generator
> shark repellent
> fishing kits
> emergency radio beacon
> de-salting tablets
> first-aid kits

Before take-off the passengers must be briefed on—

(a) releasing seat belts,
(b) protecting the face and head,
(c) order of abandoning the aircraft,
(d) inflating life jackets, and
(e) inflating and boarding the life raft.

Such a briefing is not intended to alarm the passengers; rather it is to be regarded as the airborne equivalent of lifeboat drill at sea.

Flying over Water

While flying on a typical map reading, cross country, it is standard practice to remember the wind direction, update it with the aid of smoke on the ground and keep a good lookout for fields that would make a suitable landing area in the event of engine failure. Similar precautions are equally important over the sea, but here the situation is complicated by the fact that a landing into wind may not be the best direction to choose because the effects of the sea will have to be considered. Instead of looking for large fields the pilot should keep an eye open for ships which would be in a position to effect a rescue. Since one of the first actions to be taken during a ditching procedure is the transmission of a "Mayday" call it is particularly important to be sure of the aircraft position at all times; the rescue service will need this information if they are to search in the correct area.

When an engine fails over the water a glide approach and ditching must follow. However with modern engines the most likely cause of power loss is running out of fuel and a flight should never be continued over water until the tanks are empty. It should always be borne in mind that as the lesser of two evils an engine-assisted ditching is to be preferred to a powerless one. When it is certain that land cannot be reached, plan a powered touchdown near a ship. The foregoing does not mean that a flight over open water should be regarded as some kind of self-imposed ordeal, but it is intended to emphasize the degree of pilot responsibility inseparable from the safe conduct of such flights. In the US, over a ten-year period only one ditching in five was found to have resulted from an engine failure. The others could be attributed to running out of fuel and flying into bad weather beyond the capabilities of the aircraft and/or its crew—both pilot errors.

When for any reason it becomes necessary these are the factors that have a direct bearing on the success or otherwise of a ditching—

1. Wind speed and direction.
2. Conditions of the sea.
3. Choice of ditching direction with regard to 1 and 2.
4. Aircraft ditching characteristics.
5. Pilot skill.
6. Safety equipment available.
7. Assistance available.

Items 6 and 7 have already been mentioned in the previous text.

1. WIND SPEED AND DIRECTION

Unless there is a nearby ship, streaming smoke or steam, the only indication of the surface wind velocity will be the appearance of the sea. The following table will act as a guide in assessing the strength of the wind at sea level.

Wind Speed	Appearance of Sea
Light wind	Ripples of a scaly appearance
5 kt.	Very small waves
8–10 kt.	Small waves, some with foam crests, also intermittent widespread white caps
15 kt.	Larger waves with more frequent white caps
20–28 kt.	Medium-size waves with long foam crests, profusion of white caps
30–35 kt.	Larger waves with white foam blowing in streaks across the surface in direction of the wind
Above 35 kt.	Wavecrests break into spindrift and large streaks of foam cover the sea.

Wind direction cannot be gauged by the movement of swell since wind and swell are not interrelated. However when the wind is strong enough to be of consequence during a ditching there are usually **wind lanes,** light and darker parallel stripes on the water which are particularly noticeable when looking downwind.

2. CONDITIONS OF THE SEA

The sky changes, day by day and sometimes hour by hour, usually to the accompaniment of cloud formations and other signs that are meaningful to the pilot. Likewise the sea is in a constant state of change but, unless he is also a sailor, its appearance may mean little to the average pilot. Nevertheless an understanding of the sometimes complex movement of its surface is perhaps the most important single factor to be considered during a ditching.

Swell. This is a movement of the sea resulting from past wind action, sometimes originating from a considerable distance. Throw a stone into the center of a pond. The long ripples that reach the water's edge some appreciable time later are, in miniature form, the swell.

Swell may be distorted by nearby land masses or other sea currents but since it is, in effect, the aftermath of past wind disturbances a heavy swell can exist in conditions of zero wind. Alternatively the local wind may blow across the swell, sometimes called the **primary swell** (Fig. 24).

Waves. When the wind is strong enough (see the table on page

Fig. 24. Primary swell.

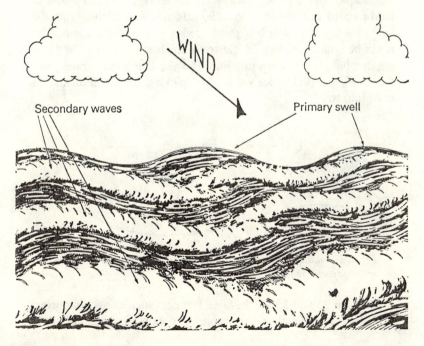

WIND

Secondary waves

Primary swell

Fig. 25. Wind causing secondary waves on the primary swell.

158) a **secondary system** of waves will be superimposed on the predominant movement of primary swell. Fig. 25 illustrates the two disturbances and it will be seen that the wind blows at 90° to the secondary system of waves, driving them across the primary swell. When the wind is of sufficient strength this secondary system may develop in size and intensity to the point where it obscures the primary swell.

Recognition from the Air. Generally the primary swell may be seen more clearly at heights of 2,000 ft. and above while the secondary waves are more recognizable below 1,000 ft.

3. CHOICE OF DITCHING DIRECTION

In a calm sea the touchdown should be made into wind. These are of course the simplest conditions for a ditching. Thinking in the usual forced landing terms, a ditching in a heavy swell may be likened to landing in an area of gently undulating sand dunes arranged in parallel lines. No one would deliberately attempt a touchdown into a raising face; where possible it would be best to land parallel to the undulations. So it is at sea. A ditching into the face of a big swell will bring with it violent deceleration and must never be attempted. Fig. 26 illustrates the best position for a ditching in wind speeds of up to 25 kt. The aim is to land parallel with the swell, for preference on a crest, picking the direction that is most into wind.

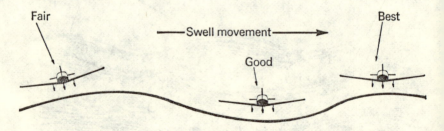

Fig. 26. Landing parallel with the swell in conditions of light to moderate wind.

Between 25 and 35 kt. the wind becomes increasingly important and it will be difficult or impossible to contain the drift. The prob-

lem is best dealt with by selecting an approach and ditching
direction that is a compromise between the two factors, i.e. head
towards the wind and land across the tops of the swell while avoiding the rising faces (Fig. 27).

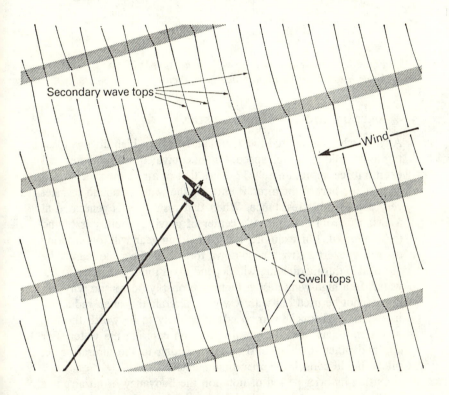

*Fig. 27. Landing across the swell and secondary waves when
the wind is between 25 and 35 knots.*

Above 35 kt. the wind is predominant. Indeed such a wind will
reduce the touchdown speed of most light single-engine aircraft to
15 kt. or less. In a high wind of this kind the swell will be shorter
and the sea is likely to be broken into a pronounced secondary
system that cannot be ignored. A ditching must then be made into
the wind and down the back of a clearly defined wave (Fig. 28).

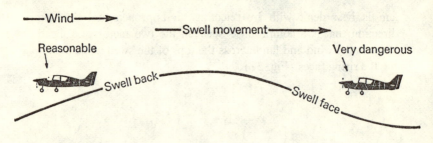

Fig. 28. Landing across the swell. Wind speeds in excess of 35 knots assume prime importance in a ditching.

4. AIRCRAFT DITCHING CHARACTERISTICS

Anyone who has entered the water badly from a high dive will testify to its solidity at high speed. On an equivalent object water will exert a force approximately 13 times that of air at the same speed so that any part of the aircraft entering the water is bound to meet very considerable resistance. When that resistance is generated at a distance from the aircraft's center of gravity, stability is bound to be affected. For example, a fixed landing gear will, on entering the water, exert a strong nose-down force. For the same reason the use of flap during ditching will depend upon their proximity to the water. In a high-wing design there is probably no reason why full flap cannot be used but with low-wing aircraft the small reduction in stalling and touchdown speeds is unlikely to be worth the risk of severe impact and structural failure on entering the water. For this and other ditching information relating to the aircraft type, pilots should consult the operating manual.

During its brief period of flotation the buoyancy of an airplane is related to the volume of airframe on the water; therefore the position of the wing is important. Experiments to determine the best airframe layout for satisfactory ditching have revealed that ideally the aircraft should have a retractable landing gear and it should be of the low mid-wing type. This arrangement would allow the fuselage to plane across the water with the wing just above the surface. After deceleration the aircraft would subside and float on the wing and the fuselage until the structure filled with water and sank. Such airplanes are rare and the nearest to this ideal would be a low-wing monoplane with a retractable landing gear, followed down the scale by a low-wing fixed landing gear, with a high-wing monoplane and fixed nosewheel landing gear offering the worst ditching characteristics. Generally the larger the aircraft the better its ability to make an emergency touchdown on water.

It should always be remembered that landplanes are made to fly, not to float. Of necessity there are many small openings in the fuselage, wings and tail surfaces and a light single-engine type may be expected to sink within thirty seconds to two minutes according to the design. It is interesting to recall that in the late 1930s when a well-known American stage personality flew the Atlantic in a Lockheed twin the problem of buoyancy in the event of ditching was resolved by filling the wings with Ping-Pong balls, an idea worthy of consideration now.

Like any forced landing there is always the risk of impact distortion of the fuselage and the possibility that as a result the door may become jammed. In the procedure listed in Part II opening the door is part of the check list. During a ditching this is of particular significance when the aircraft is of the high-wing type. Past ditchings with these aircraft have shown that after entering the water there may be a tendency to roll onto one wing tip, the fuselage will settle fairly rapidly into the water and it may be impossible to open the cabin doors against outside water pressure. As an additional means of relieving this pressure the windows should be fully open before ditching.

5. PILOT SKILL

In most cases the techniques required in dealing with the other emergencies explained in this book may fairly be described as straightforward. With the best of intentions ditching cannot be so regarded. There are the conflicting factors of wind and swell, further complicated when a secondary system of waves exists. The aircraft may be anything but ideal for entering the water, a touchdown that must be correctly positioned near a ship, if indeed there is a ship to be seen. As already mentioned ditching cannot be practiced like any other exercise; therefore success in effecting a safe ditching must revolve around the skill of the pilot.

The skillful pilot is less likely to put himself in the position of having to ditch, but when circumstances make it unavoidable he will take all the preliminary actions to safeguard his passengers, he will assess the wind and the sea correctly and then choose the best approach and ditching direction. He will position the aircraft so that the occupants are rescued with a minimum of delay and the actual touchdown will be in accordance with the advice shortly to be given. He will do it all well and therefore there is a good chance that everyone will get away with, at worst, a wetting and perhaps a few minor bruises. The indifferent pilot may do none of these things correctly. In the stress of the moment he will perhaps forget to tighten his seat belt and check his passengers', he may forget to open the doors and keep them open, he may fly into a large wave or swell, causing havoc among the occupants. This pilot may handle the situation in a way that can only end in tragedy. This is not intended to frighten the reader; it is a statement of fact and a reminder that "Safety Through Knowledge," the motto of the General Aviation Safety Committee, is particularly applicable when talking of ditching.

The Ditching

When all the preliminaries have been dealt with, the pilot must concentrate on (a) correctly positioning near a ship and (b) adopting the correct technique for alighting in the water.

A ship at speed may require half a mile to stop if it is a 5,000-ton steamer, or up to six miles when the chosen savior is a 200,000-ton tanker. Therefore it is pointless to enter the water alongside, unless the ship is stationary—and then it is equally futile to land ahead. Because the pilot can see a large ship below this does not mean that the crew are aware of his little aircraft. While the engine is still functioning it is as well to fly slowly around the ship at low level altering the power setting and (when applicable) raising the landing gear before ditching.

Technique for Alighting in the Water

This is a problem of controlling the variables of heading, speed, rate of sink, touchdown area and aircraft attitude at point of entry. In the final stages the aircraft will be at the lowest safe approach speed and in a gentle descent. The passengers will be protecting their heads and faces with rolled-up coats, etc., and the pilot should have his at the ready. The best pitch attitude for ditching is—

Retractable landing gear   5°–8° nose up
Fixed landing gear   10°–12° nose up

Here at least is something that can be practiced, estimating fuselage attitude with reference to the airspeed and the artificial horizon, because low over the water in a real emergency the horizon may be obscured by spray and the broken sea. A tail-low entry will minimize the effect of nose-down pitch when the landing gear enters the water. Correctly handled there should be a minor impact as the rear fuselage makes contact with the water followed by the main impact and severe deceleration as the nose goes below the surface where it will remain for a few seconds until the aircraft comes to a halt. The ditching will cover a comparatively modest distance over the water, to the accompaniment of considerable noise and spray, often with a tendency to swing. Here are some of the "don'ts" to be observed while ditching. They are illustrated in Fig. 29.

Don't stall or drop the aircraft into the water from a height. The human frame is not good at absorbing vertical forces and in any case the more deeply an aircraft enters the water on touchdown, the greater will be the deceleration.

Don't enter the water in a nose-down attitude. The aircraft will almost certainly dive below the surface.

Don't hold the nose too high. The tail will strike the water, force down the nose and cause the aircraft to dive.

Don't attempt a ditching at high speed. The aircraft will bounce off the water and the second arrival may be out of control.

Don't allow a wing to go down at the moment of ditching. When a wing tip enters the water the aircraft is bound to swing, possibly in the direction of a raising swell or a large wave and water can be very hard at speed! For this reason—

Don't use the wing-down method when correcting for drift. Adopt the "crabbing" technique, yawing into the required direction just before touchdown. In any case a little drift is acceptable when alighting in the water. And finally—

Don't, repeat don't, fly into the face of a large wave or rising swell. This is the biggest single hazard during the actual ditching.

Having regard to all the problems by now the reader will appreciate the value of engine power during a ditching. When the engine has failed the tasks of positioning the aircraft in relation to a ship and controlling the point of touchdown, while by no means rendered impossible, is nevertheless bound to prove more difficult.

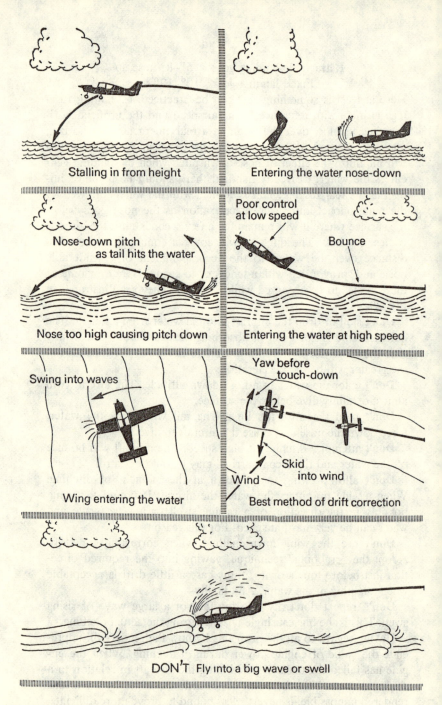

Fig. 29. *Considerations when ditching.*

Abandoning the Aircraft

Throughout the entire emergency panic must be avoided at all costs. Much will depend on the leadership displayed by the pilot. He should remember that although he is flying a small aircraft, perhaps as the holder of a Private Pilot License, he is nevertheless the captain and it is his duty to instruct the passengers and ensure that everyone knows what to do.

When the ditching has been handled correctly there should be little or no injury to the occupants and the next stage is to abandon the aircraft in an orderly manner before it sinks. It is assumed that before ditching the doors were wedged open; if not they may be jammed or held closed by outside pressure after the fuselage has entered the water. It has already been mentioned that high-wing monoplanes exhibit particular difficulties in this respect but there is the advantage that, briefly at any rate, one door may remain partly out of water as the machine rolls out onto a wingtip. If the door refuses to open a strong kick with the heels, aimed while lying across the front seats, will break the windows on the higher side of the fuselage and provide openings large enough for exit.

There are cases on record where the windshield has burst, allowing the sea to rush in, and while this will momentarily add to the general drama it has the advantage of equalizing pressure in the fuselage and assisting the opening of doors.

As soon as the aircraft has come to a halt the seat belts must be unfastened and the occupants should leave the cabin in the pre-arranged order, if necessary helping out the injured. From the accounts of those who have experienced a ditching it seems that a volume of air remains in the cabin and assists breathing but the aim should be to get out of the aircraft smartly but calmly, remembering not to kick those following behind. To assist evacuation, everything possible must be done to remove all equipment that may restrict exit from the cabin. In some ditchings considerable trouble has been caused by headsets and these must be removed from the head, unplugged and stowed away before the aircraft enters the water.

The final stage of abandonment is to inflate the life jackets and the life raft.

Entering the Life Raft

Never jump from an aircraft into a rubber dinghy or life raft—it could be damaged beyond repair. When it has inflated in the inverted position follow the instruction for righting and boarding. In the procedure listed on page 155 pilots were warned to swim or paddle away from the aircraft before it sinks. This is to avoid the risk of damage to the dinghy or personal injury through being caught by part of the sinking structure.

Survival at Sea

Should it be necessary to ditch in the open sea, away from the usual shipping lanes some time may elapse before rescue. The steps that can be taken to help search and rescue will depend upon the scale of equipment carried in the life raft (see page 156). In this situation the problem is two-fold: to attract the attention of any ship or aircraft likely to be within visual distance and to safeguard the physical condition of the survivors.

SIGNALING

Pyrotechnics will be limited; therefore save them until a ship or aircraft is seen. When lighted they must be kept well away from the life raft and the body. When an aircraft appears to be looking for survivors, or it is likely to fly nearby, use the sea marker dye to attract attention. Some emergency radio beacons have a built-in hand generator but those operated by battery power should be restricted to short periods at intervals. A small pocket mirror can make an effective signaling device when used in conjunction with the sun.

WATER

For survival, water is more important than food and in temperate climates a man requires between two and eight ounces a day—in high temperatures considerably more. Possible sources of water are rain and sea water treated with desalination tablets.

Much can be done to conserve body fluids and so reduce the water requirement—

(a) Prevent sweating in hot climates (see Keeping Cool, page 170).

(b) Reduce, or better still, cut out smoking.

(c) Eat very little to conserve the digestive fluids. Remember the body can go for long periods without food.

(d) Reduce thirst by sucking a piece of cloth or any small object such as a button.

(e) Never drink salt water or urine.

FOOD

When there is little water eat lightly. A lot of body fluid is absorbed by protein (eggs, fish, sea birds, etc.). Possible sources of food are all sea birds, also fish, but the following types are poisonous—

> brightly colored fish
> fish that "puff up"
> fish with human-looking teeth or a mouth resembling that of a parrot
> fish covered with spikes or bristles

FISHING

In the absence of bait a small piece of cloth may be used. Red is the best color. Small fish are habitual dinghy followers and they may often be caught with a makeshift net.

A fishing line can cut the hands. Use something for a reel or a handle and never attach the line to the life raft or dinghy.

Save bits of a previous catch for future bait.

Night fishing with the aid of a light can be very successful.

SHARKS

In areas where sharks, swordfish or other dangerous fish are indigenous wait until nightfall before throwing overboard waste food, or body waste.

When dangerous fish are in evidence stop fishing immediately, remain quiet, keep clothing on and never trail hands or feet in the water. An attack is then unlikely.

Should a dangerous fish appear before the survivors have boarded the dinghy or life raft, form an outward-facing circle, then beat the water vigorously and in unison.

KEEPING WARM

Keep the hands warm by placing under armpits or between thighs.

Keep clothing and dinghy dry.

Conserve body heat by keeping close together.

KEEPING COOL

Dip clothing in the sea, wring out and put on again until dry, then repeat the process.

Precautions—

(a) Ensure that clothing is dry by nightfall.

(b) Prevent salt sores by brushing off dry salt which will have accumulated on the body.

MEDICAL CARE

When there is a lot of sun take care not to expose the body needlessly, and use anti-sunburn cream if available.

Prevent sore eyes by wearing sun glasses or using a makeshift eye shield.

Avoid seasickness by keeping occupied.

Prevent sore feet by keeping the floor of the dinghy or life raft dry. Treat "immersion foot" by removing footwear, drying, wrapping the feet loosely with dry cloth and exercising the toes and feet.

Avoid general body stiffness by carrying out mild exercise, if necessary on a rotating basis with the other survivors.

Sore lips should be treated with antiseptic cream. Do not lick.

Constipation and inability to urinate must be expected when there is a shortage of food and water. This need not be a cause for concern.

CONCLUSIONS

In the United States it is unlikely that a light airplane ditching will occur very far from a busy shipping lane. This may not be the case in other parts of the world and the message is clear: You embark on such flights knowing the risks involved. The technique of ditching is one that can usually only be read about although there is sufficient past experience to provide sound guidance and advice to others. The successful outcome of a ditching calls for a cool head and pilot leadership coupled with reasonable sea conditions —but once safely in the dinghy, never give up hope of rescue.

CHAPTER 13

Landing Gear and Brake Failure

PART I. THE SITUATION

The cynic will tell you that in flying it is always the unusual that is most likely to happen. So it was with Frank, a bustling man in his early forties who within a few years had turned his RAF pension into a highly successful import business. Like so many with a flair for making money Frank would drive himself beyond all reason, working sometimes sixteen hours a day in a determined effort to expand, so that his company could be floated. On the few occasions when the strains of business entered the home his wife, trying to reason with him, would end her plea for a little restraint with the words "It's no use, Frank, you're determined to be the richest man in the cemetery." He was a fine chap really but the man suffered from a restless nature and this read across to his flying. Frank could not bear to waste time, ever. His aircraft, a fast well-equipped twin, could often be seen taking off and landing in the kind of weather that might tax the skill of an airline captain.

The trip to Holland on the day it happened produced one fiasco after another. The business contact in Rotterdam had misunderstood his appointment and was away, then his deputy tried to deal adequately with Frank without success. Somewhat disgruntled he drove back to Rotterdam Airport and on the way the rent-a-car had a puncture which proved a villain to deal with because the wheel arch was packed with frozen slush. It took an age to change the wheel in the freezing January wind and it was a pale and drawn Frank who entered the warmth of the airport building and filed a flight plan for Coventry, his home base.

A preflight check, carefully inspecting the airframe for ice, and he was off taxiing to the holding point. Earlier that day the snowplows had made a good job of clearing the runway and all that now remained was a light slush, the remnants of a subsequent gentle fall. As he expected the take-off took a little longer than usual as the dirty grey half-melted snow retarded the wheels and made a cascade in the slipstream. But once airborne in the cold, dense air the powerful twin rocketed up to cruising level where Frank changed frequency from Amsterdam Control to London. The usual cut-and-thrust on the busy radio channels seemed particularly bad that afternoon. Apparently there was a major snag at one of the international airports and they were handing out diversions and stacking instructions like trading stamps. Frank's call sign burst through the ceaseless babble—"Golf Hotel Uniform climb to Flight Level Seven-Zero and advise when level." This took him through controlled airspace, there was no delay and the rest was routine; the normal descent and joining instructions at Coventry.

Frank selected landing gear down and was exasperated more than alarmed to see the red light remain on. This was going to be the end of a perfect day; appointment that misfired, puncture on the way to the airport and now this, the threat of a wheels-up landing. He selected "wheels up" and recycled the landing gear sequence. Still the red light. There was nothing for it but to use the emergency system. It made no difference—there was that uncompromising, unblinking light, brighter than ever. They advised him to take up a hold on the "Charlie Alpha" beacon and burn off most of the fuel but it was becoming dark and rain, then sleet had reduced the visibility to the point where Frank, for all his skill, was developing an urge to get the airplane in the hangar and settle for a double Scotch. He elected to do a wheels-up landing with fire engines positioned along the runway. By now one or two of the city fire engines had arrived and were busy putting down a carpet of foam.

It was at the beginning of long finals that Frank instinctively checked "wheels down" and gave the selector a push. To his astonishment the green lights were on and he was so bemused by this odd development that until the runway lights appeared more or less directly below the nose he forgot to lower flap. As a result he touched down halfway along the landing area, immediately applied the brakes and since they had little or no effect, ran off the end of the runway into the overshoot area where he finally came to rest with one wing tip against an obstruction. He was glad to be down!

Surprisingly, perhaps, for a man of such impatient temperament, Frank was always ready to learn from his mistakes. An examination of the aircraft revealed that during the take-off at Rotterdam a good deal of slush had found its way into the rear of the landing gear bays and this had frozen after they put him up to Flight Level 70. The experts reckoned that it wasn't until he had descended below the freezing level and spent some time in the holding pattern that the ice had melted sufficiently to allow the wheels to come down on finals. That he had misjudged the approach in the heat of the situation was no secret to Frank but the brake failure he found puzzling until he recognized that it wasn't really a case of brake failure at all. He now realizes that what might be an adequate landing run on a dry runway can be thoroughly inadequate in heavy rain or slush. Thinking about it that evening it dawned on Frank that he should have been forewarned when he jacked up the car on the way to Rotterdam Airport and found the wheel arch packed with ice.

PART II. THE PROCEDURE

Landing When the Landing Gear Fails to Lock Down

Attempts to lower the landing gear by emergency means having failed (explained in Part III) a wheels-up landing is unavoidable.

1. Check seat belt tight.
2. Plan to land on the runway, not on the grass.
3. Make a normal approach using the optimum flap setting.
4. On short finals unlock the doors.

5. When it is certain the runway will be reached operate the idle cut-off, turn off the fuel and switch off the ignition and the master switch.

6. Aim to touch down in the level attitude.

FAILURE OF ONE WHEEL TO LOCK

(NOTE: with some types of aircraft it is preferable to do a wheels-up landing.)

1. Check seat belt tight.

2. Approach in the normal way using the optimum flap setting.

3. On short finals unlock the doors.

4. When it is certain the runway will be reached operate the idle cut-off, turn off the fuel and switch off the ignition and the master switch.

5. Be prepared for the aircraft to swing as the wing goes down during the landing run and plan with a view to avoiding obstructions.

6. After touchdown use aileron away from the failed landing gear leg. As the aircraft decelerates and the wing goes down use opposite brake and nosewheel steering to contain the swing.

FAILURE OF THE NOSEWHEEL TO LOCK

1. Check seat belt tight.

2. Approach in the normal way using the optimum flap setting.

3. Deliberately bounce the main wheels on the runway in an effort to free the nosewheel. Repeat the procedure several times if conditions permit. If the nosewheel refuses to lock down—

4. Fly round the pattern, join the approach and lower full flap.

5. On short finals unlock the hatches.

6. When it is certain the runway will be reached (allowing for full flap) operate the idle cut-off, turn off the fuel and switch off the ignition and the master switch.

7. Touch down in a nose-up attitude and use the elevators to hold the nosewheel off the ground for as long as possible.

8. Not until the nose makes contact with the runway may the brakes be used. Then apply the brakes to shorten the landing run.

Landing When the Brakes Are Known to Have Failed

1. Check seat belt tight.
2. If possible pick a large airfield for the emergency landing.
3. When the area is suitable, plan to land on the grass.
4. On the approach lower full flap and trim at the lowest possible airspeed consistent with safety.
5. On short finals unlock the doors.
6. Touch down at the beginning of the landing area and hold up the nose for as long as possible.
7. If it seems likely the airfield will be overrun, operate the idle cut-off, turn off the fuel and switch off the ignition and the master switch.
8. If necessary make evasive turns to avoid obstructions.

Landing on a Burst Tire

1. Check seat belt tight.
2. Plan to land on the grass if a suitable area is available.
3. Make a normal approach using full flap and trim at the lowest possible airspeed consistent with safety.
4. On short finals unlock the doors.
5. When it is certain the landing area will be reached, operate the idle cut-off, turn off the fuel and switch off the ignition and the master switch.
6. Touch down, then hold the ailerons towards the good tire.
7. As the aircraft slows down and begins to settle on the burst tire use the brakes and nosewheel steering to counteract swing towards the burst tire.

Landing on a Runway Covered with Rain, Slush or Snow

1. After ATC has given the runway state and indicated the areas to be avoided plan an approach with this in mind.
2. On short finals reduce the airspeed to the lowest consistent with safety. When landing on snow or slush avoid damaging the flaps by using the optimum setting; otherwise use full flap.
3. When the entire runway length is covered touch down near

the threshold. Allow the snow or slush to retard the aircraft to a moderate speed before applying the brakes.

4. When part of the runway is clear of snow or slush and it is long enough for a landing, use the throttle to delay touchdown until the dry area is reached.

5. While landing on a wet runway following a heavy shower, land short at a low speed and delay applying the brakes until the aircraft has slowed to a moderate speed. Never apply sufficient pressure to lock the wheels.

PART III. BACKGROUND INFORMATION

Pilots with an understanding of the operation of aircraft systems are more likely to deal successfully with an emergency caused by a mechanical fault than those with little or no knowledge; therefore the following notes on landing gear and brake systems are intended as revision. These notes can only be of a general nature and details applicable to specific aircraft types will be found in the operating manual.

Retractable Landing Gear

The function of retracting and lowering the landing gear may be performed by one of these methods—

1. Hand-operated.
2. Hydraulic system.
3. Electric system.
4. Pneumatic System.

In all cases some kind of positive "down" lock is provided to ensure that while on the ground the landing gear will remain rigidly extended. The wheels may be held retracted by a mechanical "up" lock or by hydraulic/pneumatic pressure according to the system used.

LANDING GEAR LOCK AND POSITION INDICATORS

It is common practice to use one or more green lights to indicate "wheels down and locked" but when the indicator is of the single-light type it will only come on when all wheels are correctly locked. Unfortunately there is no uniform system of indications for "wheels up" or "wheels in transit." On some aircraft there is a red light when the wheels are in transit (i.e. moving between the up and down positions) and no light after the landing gear has locked up, while many of the modern light twins show no lights while the wheels are in transit and an amber light for "up." Yet another warning system is that used on the Piper PA 39 Twin Comanche where the usual green light confirms "locked down," a white light shows "wheels in transit" and an amber light denotes "wheels locked up." From this it will be seen that other than green for "locked down," landing gear warning systems differ from one design to another and it is particularly important that pilots should fully understand the lights on the aircraft type being flown. Often the warning lights are of the "press-to-test" type and for night flying their intensity is automatically dimmed when the navigation lights are on.

Some aircraft have an additional down lock warning, a mechanical indicator that protrudes above the wing surface when the wheels are locked ready for landing.

SAFEGUARDS

To prevent inadvertent retraction of the landing gear while the aircraft is on the ground the selector is provided with a device that requires a positive effort to override. Additionally most modern aircraft have a limit valve or switch which prevents the retraction circuit from operating while the weight of the aircraft is supported on the ground. The limit valve or switch is fitted to one of the telescopic landing gear struts and is set to cut out after lift-off.

The risk of inadvertently landing with the landing gear retracted has existed since the invention itself. The design features adopted to try and avoid such an accident vary according to aircraft type, some of the methods in use being—

1. Automatic lowering of the landing gear when power and airspeed are reduced below a certain level.

2. Flashing warning lights. Often the amber "up" light is used for the purpose but sometimes there is a separate red light on or near the landing gear selector.

3. A warning horn which like the warning light operates when the throttle(s) are brought back below a particular setting, usually 12 in. manifold pressure.

Hydraulic Systems

The principles of hydraulics offer the engineer a convenient method of transmitting power around difficult corners to inaccessible places through a system of small diameter high-pressure pipes filled with fluid, usually a mineral-based oil. Oil has the advantage of possessing low friction and resistance to freezing while for all practical purposes it is incompressible.

The heart of an aircraft hydraulic system is an **engine-driven pump** fed by a **reservoir** containing the hydraulic fluid. Pressure from the pump is led via the main feed to the **selectors** controlling the landing gear, flaps and perhaps other services (e.g. air stairs). In effect these selectors are three-position valves which control the hydraulic fluid thus: "up," "neutral or idle" and "down." In the idle position pressure oil flows from the pump, through the selector valve, and returns to the reservoir. When a selection is made pressure oil is diverted to the service required filling one side of an **hydraulic jack** and moving its piston in the direction relevant to the particular function, e.g. landing gear down, flaps up, etc. Fig. 30 shows a simple hydraulic system capable of operating a retractable landing gear. It will be seen that the piston in the hydraulic jack is two-sided so that fluid may be pumped in either direction to effect "up" or "down." When the jack is in operation oil from the non-pressure side of the piston will return through the selector to the reservoir. When the jack has performed its function, and in so doing reached the end of its travel, back pressure within the hydraulic line under pressure will return the selector to neutral so that the engine-driven pump may idle again until the next selection is made. This refinement is not shown in the diagram.

Although most hydraulic pumps are coupled directly to the engine some aircraft have an electro-hydraulic system where the pump is driven by an electric motor. A blown fuse or circuit breaker will, in these systems, render the hydraulic services inoperative.

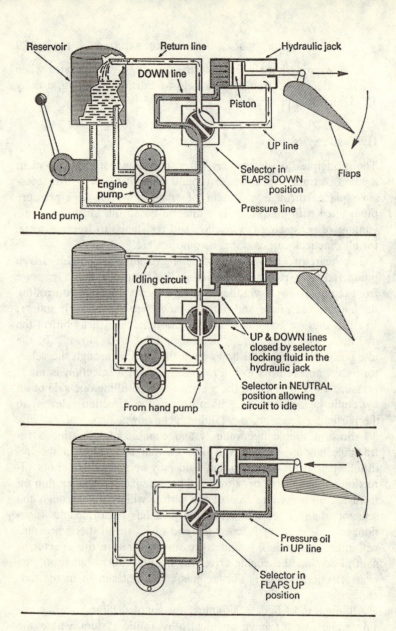

Fig. 30. Basic hydraulic circuit.

*Top illustration shows selector in the "flaps down" position.
Next picture illustrates circuit in the idling phase (flaps locked
down) and the last diagram shows the flap being raised.*

EMERGENCY LOWERING OF HYDRAULIC LANDING GEAR

The faults that may occur with hydraulic systems and the provisions made to rectify them are described below.

1. *Loss of Hydraulic Fluid.* A leaking joint or fractured pipe from the selector to one of the jacks may not affect the other services but the danger of this situation is serious loss of hydraulic fluid. To cater for this eventuality the lower portion of the reservoir is designed to retain an emergency fluid supply which can only be drawn by an independent hand pump. Assuming that "flaps down" had been selected without effect, the landing gear should then be tried. If this too will not move then either the engine-driven pump is inoperative or there is a leak in the "flaps down" line through which most of the hydraulic fluid has been lost. However it should still be possible to operate the landing gear and "flaps up" by using the hand pump.

2. *Failure of the Engine-driven Pump.* This fault will be confirmed by the refusal of any hydraulic service to operate. The hand pump will then have to be used.

3. *Landing Gear Moves Up or Down but Refuses to Lock.* Selectors of the type that return automatically to neutral at the completion of a function are adjusted to do so at a particular hydraulic pressure. If for any reason the idle circuit valve is set at too low a pressure it is sometimes the case that the selector will "blow back" to neutral before the landing gear has locked. When this occurs the selector lever may be held in the required position until the relevant warning light confirms "locked" (up or down) when it must be released immediately to avoid excessive pressure in the hydraulic circuit. Should these measures fail it is possible that something is fouling one of the wheel retraction linkages and in the case of a nosewheel the "bouncing" procedure outlined on page 174 should be adopted in an effort to dislodge the cause of the trouble.

4. *Inability to Lower the Landing Gear by Engine or Hand Pump.* This situation is usually accompanied by the complete loss of hydraulic services so that almost certainly the flaps will be inoperative for the landing. In this case the prime objective is to get the wheels down and locked and the emergency system provided for the purpose usually takes the form of a compressed air

or CO_2 bottle which may be discharged into the "down" side of the landing gear jacks (in most aircraft there is one jack for each landing gear leg). In so doing a valve isolates the normal hydraulic lines to prevent loss of emergency air pressure through a possible pipe fracture. This emergency system is confined to the landing gear and cannot be used for lowering the flaps. After the emergency system has been used the landing gear must be left down in the event of an overshoot.

Electric Systems

General information on aircraft electric circuits was given in Chapter 8 (page 87). This section is confined to electrically operated landing gear. These are to be found on a number of light single- and twin-engine designs. The principle is that when a selection is made, say, "wheels up," current from the main circuit is directed to an electric motor which drives a retraction assembly comprising a gear train and screw jack. Push-pull rods connect the retraction assembly to the nosewheel and main wheels and a limit switch installed on one landing gear leg prevents accidental retraction so long as the weight of the aircraft is supported by the ground.

EMERGENCY LOWERING OF ELECTRIC LANDING GEAR

Failure of the lowering sequence may result from—
    (a) a blown fuse of circuit breaker,
    (b) a damaged selector or circuit,
    (c) a mechanical fault in the retraction assembly or linkage to the landing gear, or
    (d) a burned-out electric motor.

Fault (a) may be rectifiable but if the circuit continues to blow this could be as a result of fault (c). The retraction assembly is usually under an easily removable access panel situated on the floor within reach of the pilot and it may be possible to see obvious signs of blockage fouling the gears or the associated screw jack. When efforts to lower the landing gear by normal means have failed the emergency procedure will have to be adopted, details of which are in the operating manual and on the inside of the retraction assembly cover plate.

The usual procedure is to disengage the landing gear push-pull rods from the retraction assembly (using the lever marked for the purpose) thus leaving the landing gear free to be moved manually, an operation effected by inserting a long bar (stowed in the retraction assembly compartment) into a socket, then moving it in the direction indicated. When the landing gear is fully lowered it will be made safe for landing by the "down" locks.

Pneumatic Systems

The pneumatic operation of flaps, brakes and landing gear is now uncommon although the Hawker Siddely Dove which uses this type of system is still flying in fairly considerable numbers. In essence a pneumatic system is rather similar to the hydraulic circuit described on page 179, except that in place of the hydraulic fluid and the reservoir is a cylinder holding compressed air at a pressure of between 400 and 1,000 psi. Pressure is maintained by one or more engine-driven compressors and the pressure air is fed via **filters** and a **water trap** (to extract moisture collected from the atmosphere) to the selector valves controlling landing gear retraction, flaps and the brakes. A **triple pressure gauge** situated on the instrument panel provides the following information—

Center finger   pressure in the system
Left finger   pressure to left brake
Right finger   pressure to right brake

Operation of the brakes is described on page 186.

EMERGENCY LOWERING OF PNEUMATIC LANDING GEAR

When the normal system fails to lower, the landing gear reference to the central finger on the triple pressure gauge will determine whether or not the fault is due to low or complete lack of pressure. After heavy and prolonged braking or repeated use of the flaps and landing gear during circuit flying a faulty pneumatic system may fail to maintain the required minimum pressure. Often it is only a matter of allowing a little more time for the pressure to build up before the landing gear may be lowered in the normal way.

If the main system should fail there is an independent compressed-air bottle provided and the instruction for emergency lowering of the landing gear will be found in the operating manual. In the HS Dove these instructions are shown on a plate affixed to the control column.

Preliminary Actions When the Landing Gear Refuses to Lower Correctly

Before a decision is made to implement the various procedures listed in Part II of this chapter Air Traffic Control should be warned of the difficulty. The airfield will then be alerted and so be able to advise on the best landing area, but if all possible precautions are to be completed before the wheels-up landing (warning other traffic, fire service alert, foam on the runway, etc.) the pilot will have to transmit his emergency message as soon as there is a risk of belly landing. Even at this stage there are additional steps that can be taken to get the wheels down and locked. When the green indicator fails to light, the wheels should be raised, then lowered again to recycle the system, but even when the fault persists it may be nothing more serious than a burned-out indicator bulb or a faulty landing gear micro-switch. The indicator bulb can usually be tested by pressing or sometimes there is an alternative bulb, but when the landing gear cannot be seen from the cabin and satisfactory operation of the down locks is in doubt a low and slow fly past, using the optimum flap setting, should be made close to the control tower so that an external report can be made. If advised that the landing gear appears to be locked down the next stage is to confirm this by touching the wheels firmly on the runway at a low approach speed without allowing the full weight of the aircraft to settle on the landing gear. At this stage, provided the landing gear feels firm and the runway is long enough, it should be possible to close the throttle(s) and gently bring the aircraft to a halt. When there are obvious signs of the landing gear collapsing it is best to go round again so that the full crash check procedure may be completed. It has already been mentioned in Part II that whenever possible an airfield with a long runway should be chosen for the emergency.

When the indications, either within the aircraft or from a ground observation, are that the wheels are partly down but not locked these additional steps may be taken in an endeavor to move the landing gear to the fully extended position. It is assumed that by now all emergency lowering systems have been tried without success.

1. *Rocking the Wings*. This has been known to assist in moving the landing gear into the locking phase.

2. *Application of "g."* By diving to a speed slightly above normal cruising and pulling up to the point where vision is beginning to darken (grey-out) a stubborn landing gear can often be persuaded to lock down.

The Wheels-up Landing

When all measures have failed to lower the landing gear a wheels-up landing will have to be carried out following the procedures explained on page 174. It will be noted that in some of these procedures use of part flap only is recommended. This is to protect them from unnecessary damage during the wheels-up touchdown. In the case of a high-wing monoplane, full flap may be used since the flaps will be well clear of the ground.

Experience has shown that less damage is caused to an aircraft when a wheels-up landing is performed on a runway, rather than on grass—where there is a tendency to dig in.

Although the fire departments should have been alerted the actual risk of fire or indeed serious airframe damage of any kind is slight, provided the situation is handled correctly and a touchdown is made in the level attitude.

PARTIAL FAILURE TO LOCK

When the landing gear fault is confined to one main leg it may still be possible to land on the nosewheel and the other main wheel. However some aircraft are best landed with all wheels locked or all wheels retracted and the operating manual or if necessary the manufacturers should be consulted for advice on a particular type. Provided the main wheels are locked down landing with a failed nosewheel should prove less of a problem.

Aircraft Braking Systems

Aircraft brakes may be operated by one of the following methods—

1. Mechanical effort.
2. Pneumatic pressure.
3. Hydraulic pressure.

MECHANICAL BRAKES

Cable-operated mechanical brakes of the drum and expanding shoe type are confined to aircraft of older design. The brakes are applied either through heel pedals situated near the rudder control or by a hand lever acting through a **differential unit** linked to the rudder pedals. In either case one wheel may be made to apply greater braking effort than the other to assist steering while taxiing. The main weakness with this type of system is that the drums tend to retain friction-generated heat and the brake will "fade." Furthermore the cable/brake shoe operation requires constant adjustment if the limited efficiency of this type of system is to be maintained. Cable-operated brakes of this kind are most likely to fade while being used to taxi a tailwheel aircraft in a strong cross wind —the very time when they are most needed.

PNEUMATIC BRAKES

Like mechanical brakes the pneumatic system is now only to be seen on older types of aircraft. In the past, pneumatic brakes were fitted to larger civil aircraft and most of the military advanced trainers and operational types.

The pneumatic system described on page 183 supplies pressure air to a **dual relay valve,** a unit comprised of two pressure air controllers, one for each brake. The brakes are applied by a hand grip conveniently positioned on the control stick or wheel and there is a lever locking device for parking. When the lever is squeezed compressed air flows from the dual relay valve supplying equal pressure to the wheel units where rubber sacks similar in appearance to small inner tubes inflate, pressing the brake shoes against the drums which in turn provide the necessary braking action. Through the action of a differential linkage, application of left or right rudder will cause the dual relay valve to increase brake pressure in the same sense, i.e. left rudder, more left brake, while compressed air is allowed to escape from the starboard wheel unit which in this case is on the outside of the resultant turn. When the aircraft is parked in windy conditions the action of the differential unit will exhaust the supply of pressure air unless the rudder is prevented from moving by operating the control locks. While some pneumatic brake systems are very effective, like all drum/ brake shoe installations there is the problem of fading at the very time when maximum efficiency is needed.

HYDRAULIC BRAKES

Practically without exception modern aircraft are fitted with disc brakes, a type of braking unit that was originally developed for airplanes and which only later found favor on the automobile. The most common method of application is through toe pedals fitted to the rudder control, with a separate parking knob or handle. There are, however, many aircraft where the brakes are operated by a hand lever and while some of these incorporate differential braking through the rudder pedals others provide braking in unison only. These systems are very simple indeed. When the brakes are applied, pressure oil is fed to slave cylinders on the wheel units which press composition pads onto a cast-iron disc fixed to the landing wheel. There are two or more pads applying pressure to both sides of the disc in a squeezing action. Being exposed to the air, heat generated through braking is allowed to dissipate rapidly and as a result fading is almost completely eliminated. On smaller aircraft the brake system is a self-contained unit independent of the main hydraulic circuit. A simplified hydraulic brake system is shown in Fig. 31.

During the preflight inspection all brake connections, whatever the system, should be inspected for obvious signs of damage. In the case of hydraulic brakes there should be no evidence of oil leaking from the various joints. An oil leak is likely to run down and drip from the lower point on the hydraulic flexible hose.

LOSS OF BRAKING EFFICIENCY

It is almost unknown for modern aircraft brakes to fail but the procedure to adopt on these rare occasions is explained on page 176. More likely is the possibility of impaired braking efficiency due to rain, slush, snow or ice on the runway. The danger is of growing importance, now that light aircraft are operating in IFR with increasing frequency. While the effects of ice and snow are

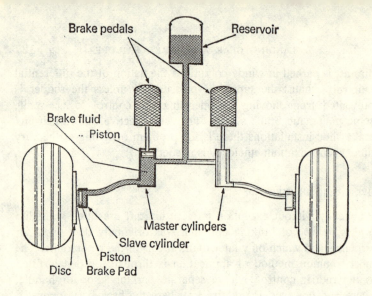

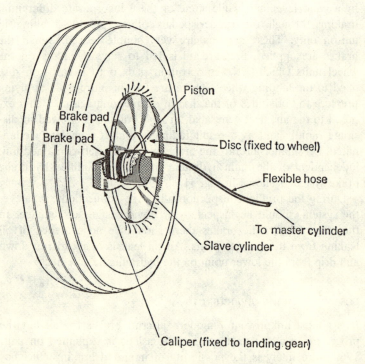

Fig. 31. Simple hydraulic brake system.

Lower diagram shows a typical single-piston disc unit of the type used on most light aircraft.

well-known driving hazards, most pilots are unaware of the possible dangers of landing on a very wet runway. Following several unexplained accidents when large transport aircraft with serviceable brakes departed the end of the runway, experiments revealed that when a rain thickness of more than 0.2 in. (5 mm) is standing on the runway there is a tendency for a wedge of water to build up beneath the tire. Under these conditions the water may boil and emulsify the rubber. The resistance from this wedge has a vertical component powerful enough to lift the aircraft fractionally and decrease the area of tire in contact with the runway. Once formed the wedge will persist over parts of the runway carrying a water thickness considerably less than 0.2 in. In these conditions the aircraft is said to be **aquaplaning** and because of the minimal or even complete loss of tire/runway contact braking effort is seriously reduced or lost completely. There is a direct relationship between risk of aquaplaning and tire pressure, i.e. the higher the pressure, the higher the speed required to initiate the phenomenon. For example, when the main wheel tire pressure is 40 lb./sq. in. the application of brake at any speed above a modest 54 kt. will induce aquaplaning.* When flying an aircraft with a relatively high touchdown speed pilots should be aware that after a heavy rainfall has occurred braking efficiency may be impaired and hence a longer than usual landing run will be necessary. On request Air Traffic Control will give the runway state in plain language, e.g. good, medium or poor braking conditions, together with the locality and extent of water coverage. When a runway is contaminated with ice or snow this advice will be given automatically.

Putting this chapter into perspective it should be understood that in the mechanical sense, landing gear failure is rare and usually confined to a collapsed nosewheel strut. Brake failure is even more uncommon and inability to stop is almost invariably a matter of lost tire adhesion. When a landing gear exhibits signs of temperament some of the actions suggested in Part III may well provide that little extra energy needed to lock the wheels safely down but when all else has failed and a wheels-up landing is unavoidable it may be tackled with confidence by avoiding Frank's mistakes with the air of a little more planning. They say the next field is always greener but this is not true when getting there entails running the airplane off the airfield.

---

* Minimum speed for the onset of aquaplaning is 8.6 × square root of the tire pressure in lb./sq. in.

PREDOMINANT TYPES OF ACCIDENT AND PHASE OF OPERATION IN ACCIDENTS INVOLVING PRIVATE PILOT LICENCE HOLDERS IN GREAT BRITAIN

1960–70 INCLUSIVE

PHASE OF OPERATION

Notifiable Accidents (643)   %
1. Landing Run   169   26
2. Final Approach   112   17
3. En-route Cruise   109   17
4. Initial Climb   95   15
5. General/Others   73   11
6. Take-off Run   58   9
7. Initial Approach   57   4

Fatal Accidents (90)   %
1. En-route Cruise   31   34
2. General/Others   25   28
3. Initial Climb   16   18
4. Initial Approach   9   10
5. Final Approach   8   9
6. Landing Run   1   1
7. Take-off Run   0   0

PHASE OF OPERATION

Type of Accident

Notifiable Accidents (636)

		%
1. Heavy Landing	106	17
2. Nose-over	84	13
3. Unintentional Spin/Stall	79	12
4. Landing Gear Collapsed	62	10
5. Ground Loop	46	7
6. Over Run	44	7
7. Collision with Trees	38	6
8. Undershoot	35	5
9. Other Forms, Loss of Control in Air	27	4
10. Collision with Level Ground/Water	24	4
11. Collision with Other Objects	22	3
12. Wheels-up Landing	21	3
13. Collision with High Ground	17	3
14. Collision with Wires/Poles	17	3
15. Intentional Spin/Stall	7	1
16. Airframe Failure in Air	7	1

Fatal Accidents (84)

		%
1. Unintentional Spin/Stall	28	33
2. Collision with High Ground	14	17
3. Collision with Level Ground/Water	13	15
4. Collision with Trees	6	7
5. Collision with Wires/Poles	5	6
6. Intentional Spin/Stall	4	5
7. Other Forms, Loss of Control in Air	4	5
8. Airframe Failure in Air	4	5
9. Collision with Other Objects	2	2
10. Undershoot	2	2
11. Heavy Landing	1	1
12. Nose-over	1	1